Energetic Invocations Series:

A Book of Vibrational Change - Volumes 1-17

Parts One to Five, with Process This

Julie Bonetti and Susan Barbaro

Copyright © 2016 by Julie Bonetti and Susan Barbaro
The material, in each series, is based upon *Energetic Invocations: A Book of Vibrational Change* ©2015, by Julie Bonetti and Susan Barbaro, and includes all parts with Process This components.

ISBN-13: 978-0-9861401-5-0
ISBN-10: 0-9861401-5-5

All rights reserved. No part of this book may be reproduced or transmitted in any form or by any means, electronic or mechanical, including photocopying, recording, or by any information storage and retrieval system without permission in writing from the authors.

Printed in the United States of America
Cover Photos, Art and Design by Julie Bonetti and Susan Barbaro, ©2016
Published by EI Alliance

EnergeticInvocations@gmail.com or visit https://fanlink.tv/EiAlliance

No AI was used to create, develop, research, write or produce this book.

Disclaimer: The authors of this book do not dispense medical advice or prescribe any technique as a form of treatment for physical, emotional or mental problems. The authors encourage all to obtain the expertise and medical advice of a trusted physician, therapist or practitioner, as is appropriate. The intent of the authors is to share information of a general nature to possibly assist in others' quest for change. In the event others use any of the information in this book for themselves the authors and the publisher assume no responsibility for their actions. This book is a work of nonfiction and the authors have selected what to include based on their own perspective and life experiences. Any names and identifying details of individuals used to illustrate examples have been changed and do not refer to any one specific individual or entity.

FROM EI ALLIANCE, BY JULIE BONETTI AND SUSAN BARBARO

Energetic Invocations: A Book of Vibrational Change

Energetic Invocations Series: A Book of Vibrational Change - Volumes 1-17

How Do I Live When I Don't Fit In? A Self-Reflective Journal

The Endra Scripts - Endra: Anecdotes of a Modern Day Witch -Phases 1 – 10
(Pseudonym: Polonious)

Conversations with an Extra Terrestrial - The Mitsu Quadrilogy
(Pseudonym: Polonious)

Think You Know "The Kybalion?"

How to Buy the Perfect Gift, Using Numerology

How Trump Wins

Donald J. Trump: Do you stand with him? Who does he stand with?
The Science and Energy Behind Trump

the List

Christmas & Holiday Trivia – Volume 1 & Volume 2

Dear Drew

"I'm afraid of the dark" and other children's voices

And So, I Pray

BLOTCH© cards and ebooks

And more!

Plus these archived Podcast Shows:
So What! Now What?
Write, Now! with Julie B
Your Presence Is Required
Let's Talk About Energy, Ours & Yours
The Kybalion: A Conversation
Ancient Texts – The Genealogy of Energy
Oprah! Can You Hear Me? Oprah vs. Donald 2020 and Beyond!

And visit: https://fanlink.tv/EiAlliance

***

*This is dedicated
to all the abused, bullied children and adults
who keep saying
something has to change.*

Hopefully this helps to create this change.

*Because,
the only way to change the world
is to change your world.*

Table of Contents

To the Reader   *Survivor/Creator*

Energetic Invocations Overview   *Vibrations*

Part One: Self   *Page 17*
Volume 1: Who I Am?   *Worth*
Volume 2: How do I exhibit self-care?   *Happiness*
Volume 3: What is it like to be healthy?   *Influence/Charity*

Part Two: Journey   *Page 47*
Volume 4: How do I choose to live my life?   *Gratitude/Guilt*
Volume 5: What can I create with my expertise? *Patterns*
Volume 6: What is my currency?   *Essence*
Volume 7: What is my level of commitment?   *Passion*
Volume 8: What can my experience do for me? *Possibility*

Part Three: People   *Page 88*
Volume 9: How do I perceive relationships?   *Intent*
Volume 10: Will love make me whole?   *Wholeness*
Volume 11: Who are the people like me?   *Predictability*

Part Four: Environment   *Page 120*
Volume 12: How do I flourish in my environment? *Space*
Volume 13: Is there a definition for happiness? *Productivity*
Volume 14: Where do I fuel my presence?   *Enrichment*

Part Five: World   *Page 146*
Volume 15: When do I measure time?   *Nurture*
Volume 16: How do I stay balanced in the real world? *Harmony*
Volume 17: What is the truth?   *Awareness*

Final Words   *Authenticity*

To the Reader   *Survivor/Creator*

Why are you here, on this page, reading this? And why are you breathing, living on this planet? These are questions only you can answer. Yet, are we not here together, on this planet, to help each other find answers to questions like these? The true answers are within you, but the more you try to fit in, the more you lose sight of your truth.

So, are you just trying to fit in or do you really want to find your truth? We are all here and in one way or another we are all searching. The question isn't why you are searching but rather what it is that you are searching for, and that is a question only you can answer.

People think they are searching to fit in. But the truth is we are searching for who we really are. And that means something different for everyone. We want to be ourselves but are we? And as we struggle, we wonder why we are not happy.

This book will help you find your truths. It might make your head spin a little from the vibration of its words and it might pull the ground out from under you as it energizes and empowers you. It is highly laced with energy, and you will feel it. So as you open yourself up to more clarity, you may feel light headed or as if your head is swimming. Readers have shared that these kinds of experiences occur and have told us that the energy they find themselves within is powerful.

So we implore you don't read this book:
- if you aren't willing to do the work,
- if you haven't said that something has to change, and
- if you don't want to change the world.

You will not like this book if you would rather live the facade you have been living. But that isn't our problem or concern because this book isn't for everyone but you aren't everyone.

This book isn't for you:
- if you aren't open to challenging yourself, and
- if you aren't eager to confront and combat the so-called demons to set the truth free.

This book was written for those of you who find it, get it, and with the understanding of what is within it, become your own Guru. Unlike 'How To' books with pat answers and trite quotes that are difficult to fully absorb and put to use, this book will act as a guide, offering opportunities just for you, to open up something new. Isn't it time for the you who has been cowering in the shadows of everyone else, the you who has been trudging along knowing something is wrong, and the you who has been fighting so-called demons just to get through the day, to do the work and change your world? This book is for You who is finally ready to get it and who is finally ready to create change.

Change occurs when you change. Most of us want to be in control and don't like the idea of change. We don't want to change our jobs, our partners, our habits, our families, our interests, even the sports teams for which we cheer. In many cases, we get comfortable in our cycles of dysfunction. We all want to feel like we belong and fit in. But what if that is not our real nature? What if we were truly to be like nature itself and change along with the seasons of the year?

What would change mean for you? Life is constantly changing, whether you see it or not. The cosmic realm itself is violent and ever changing yet that change creates expansion and growth, throughout our world and the universe. So how would your life change, if you started to see all the changes around you? What if aliens are proven to be real, how would everything change then? What would happen and what chaos would ensue? At some point, you have to resign yourself to the fact that change is going to happen. You are here and change is truly happening all around you. So, why wouldn't you be changing too?

We believe when you fully embrace this change fear takes a backseat and you yourself can expand and grow into who you can truly be. All the answers truly lie within you and you will certainly find all the answers you need by doing the work. We have done the work and have found our answers within. We are sharing our process because it is important, for in doing the work we became our own Guru. Armed with truth, we started exhibiting extreme self-care as we mapped out a new, empowering way to live, grow and think. You too can do the work, find your truth and achieve the same.

<u>Process this:</u>

A pregnant patient came to see us because she was troubled by her history of having post due date deliveries with complications. Although her children were healthy, the late deliveries created complications such as hypertension, increased heart rate and heavier birth weights. Her due date for this child was arriving and she was stressed thinking she would have similar complications. After two sessions of treatment with us, she moved into a healthier space of acknowledging that her defined due date differed from what the medical tests stated. Once she acknowledged this truth she became comfortable with that change. That very night she went home, relaxed into her changed understanding, and the next morning had a delivery that was not traumatic, with no complications.

In being open minded to anything you believe you can create change. But where do you start? First, stop looking and instead start thinking outside the box. As the box represents the norms and limitations of society, thinking outside helps you venture deeply within a new understanding. The box is also the need to fit in and has been defined by what has been okayed by everyone else. Eventually becoming one with the box, you no longer focus upon the external as you find a greater internal awareness of who you are and then begin to operate from that in a powerful way. It is difficult to be the one person who stands alone, thinking differently than everybody else. However, in many cases you already are, and are paying the price for being that way.

Those people deciding what is okay for everyone else are most often carrying dysfunction. It is time to be truly yourself and make being yourself your own okay. So now, ask yourself what you know, for then your knowledge within will reveal itself. Although you may at first doubt that you are smart enough to know what you know or don't know, wisdom will rise to your surface. Even if you feel you aren't worthy enough, thin enough, tall enough, athletic enough, pretty enough, musical enough, artistic enough, etc., once you open to doing the work you will realize there is no 'enough' that could contain You. By You, we mean all of you: your highest and best self, the You that is connected to the All. Some might define it as your soul. Trust what you feel when you read You.

The slightest awareness of the truth of you being more than 'enough' will move you, as you continue to do the work, reach more clarity and act as your own Guru. For, no Guru can match the answers that are within you. Why would you need a Guru when you have all the answers? For you truly do! Once you understand all the power you need is within, you can change anything you want to change and your truth becomes clearer. So what are you waiting for?

- What's the catch? You will get all you need, to the extent you work on you. Nobody else, not even we can tell you your truth. We are simply guides showing you the steps, but we cannot do the work you must do. You must do it, for your own sake. You are worth it and the journey is worth it.

Life is a journey and your decision to do the work is your own destiny to fulfill. Utilize this book to help push you along as you investigate the energies surrounding and affecting you, your environment and all your efforts to reach your dreams and desires. Realize you are done with the doing of your past that has only kept you stuck. For when you stop doing the same things that have been giving you the same results you start to move into something different and better. By focusing on a new conversation, you help yourself remember who you truly are. And isn't it time you released all that doesn't matter in your life so you could start focusing on what does matter?

Be honest about it or don't waste your time. There is no hidden secret, no special university and no holistic club. The truth is within you waiting to be set free. Do the work as we did, uncover your truth, learn, grow and heal. Persistently challenge yourself and focus on self-care. This doesn't mean being selfish. It means taking the time to listen, trust and have confidence in the wisdom of your inner self. Even if you only get this in concept, you are still ready to challenge yourself by working with this book. The smallest bit of awareness exhibits that a wealth of courage is just waiting to create change.

Show up for yourself. What does that mean? It means to treat yourself as if you are your own best friend. Think of all the other people you have shown up for with compassion. It is time to do that for you, methodically, introspectively, and compassionately. Reclaim your life, your truest and highest You, with integrity and respect. This goes against everything we have ever been told, including religious dogma, but it is time to question everything.

You are ready for this book:
- •if you get that something is missing from your life,
- •if you find your work and social environment not very fulfilling, and
- •if the people around you and within your world are not empowering you to be your best.

Do the work with this book, find answers within, learn, grow, share and purposefully move onward with gratitude. We continue to do this but that is our business not yours. Who you are, the work you do with this book and how it changes your world is your business. Understand that when you live focusing on your own business, your life shows up. We are clear about this, you must be too. Instead of just surviving, show up and consistently remember that You truly do matter.

Energetic Invocations Overview   *Vibrations*

You are here. You are whole. You are complete. Do you believe that?

You are also energy. Science has proven that we come from the stars so why do we often only consider ourselves as skin, bone, cells, blood, and finite? Western medicine focuses on the chemical nature of our being and ignores the electrical part of ourselves. Even science shows that there is an electrical piece of our body that is being ignored, and has shown that a heart removed from the body still beats. That is proof of energy in action. We are energy in action. And there is science behind all of this energy. Yet, the importance of all of us as energetic beings has been lost. It is truly time to embrace it.

As an energetic being, you are perfect just as you are. And once you start to deeply understand that, you can make room for the truth. So how do you do that?

Start by looking at your beliefs and asking:

- What have I been told by those around me?
- What have I been told by society as a whole?

- *What are my beliefs and most importantly, are they truly mine?*

If you have been living and implementing these beliefs, you may ask: "Why is nothing working?" Nothing is working because your space may be cluttered with self-limiting, disconnecting beliefs.

Now ask yourself:

- Have I chosen these beliefs or were they imposed upon me?

- Are those around me caught in the same vicious cycle of beliefs?
- Why do I continue to have these same beliefs if they keep me stuck?

- *What are my true beliefs?*

<u>Process this:</u>

> Have you ever waited in a long line at a store, bank, or public service, while the person behind the counter seemed to control the situation? Waiting and waiting and waiting makes you feel powerless and angry. When the clerk miserably wavers about what s/he can or cannot do to assist you, you fall into rage. The minute you do, you give into the illusion of control, and you believe you are powerless. Yet, the most powerless one of all is actually the one that believes s/he has the control. You are there to achieve your goal of some service or problem resolution and that will occur. What does anything else matter? The line will move, as will you, and you will reach your goal, regardless of what the clerk believes. There is nothing and no one here to control, except for your perception, focus and belief.

So, do you even know what you believe? Or what a belief is? Do you have the awareness to understand that beliefs have been imposed upon you and you are acting and reacting to them? Many people are not even aware of their beliefs until they are pointed out to them. If no one is pointing them out to you it is time for you to challenge yourself. Begin to define your beliefs and ask yourself if they are really yours or if you are living your life based upon someone else's beliefs? Often, beliefs are acquired from others and are based upon conditions that are not truly your own but for some reason have been adopted by you. In turn, these beliefs become magical spells that consistently lock you into an habitual struggle which suffocates your truth.

It is hard to imagine, but you could be living a life that has been fabricated by someone else's beliefs or those of society. If you are happy being in that situation then all the more power to you. But, chances are you feel miserably trapped in an unfulfilled existence where you are busy fighting so-called demons while turning to harmful things just to satisfy an emptiness that keeps screaming out for change.

Our society is not supportive. There is a never ending stream of social media, gurus, medical practitioners, and self-help books that all emphasize someone else is having this great life, because they found happiness. How come you haven't found happiness? And so now begins the greater tailspin into a darker depth of emptiness where you ask yourself:

- *Why can't I find happiness?*

Face it, it is an overwhelmingly frustrating struggle to fix everything, make things work and just fit in. No matter how hard you try you could still feel disconnected, left out, unworthy and surrounded by lack. As self-care drops to the bottom of your to do list, you may feel sick and tired. Addictive and reckless behavior could lead to self-mutilation, alcoholism, gambling, anorexia, or bouts of severe depression, and you might fall terminally ill. Failing to search inside yourself for answers may have you finding pain being comfortable and familiar.

Process this:

Have you ever lost your job or gotten laid off? In this day and age, most of us have, many times. And then the troubles seem to multiply as your rent increases, bills pile up, and friends complain that you don't join them for drinks anymore. You can't, you are worried about money and stressed out about what to do! You believe no one has any idea what you are going through and that no one cares. Feeling disconnected, sad, and angry, you may spiral into thoughts of self-destruction or worse. These moments occur for all of us, and when we are the most vulnerable we feel a disconnection from everyone and everything. But these moments are also the times when powerful energy is waking up within, challenging us to make a change. But that would mean you move from the comfort of the pain you know to something new that is undefined. Can you really be comfortable in that new discomfort?

If you can understand that and accept that, you will come to a different, healthier space. So change your perception of the situation you are in and of your world, and remember Mahatma Gandhi's words that the only way to change anything is to be the change. For, in being the change, wouldn't it follow that you end up changing your world, and in turn, *the world*?

- Instead of nourishing lack with counterproductive, self-destructive, addictive behavior, understand what you are feeling could be a reaction to what others are deciding for you.
- Rather than harming yourself, others or the environment, understand that all you need to do is to say NO to others' beliefs.
- Rather than focusing on feelings of unhappiness, choose You. Choose You and your beliefs.
- Find your own truth and listen to it.

By cleaning up your own dysfunction and operating from strength and abundance rather than weakness and lack, you become an important model for others. By stepping into what is healthy for you, rather than looking outside for solutions, you powerfully reclaim your life as you trust yourself more. By conscientiously asking: "How do I change myself?" rather than "What is someone else going to change for me?" you move victoriously ahead.

Process this:

We, the authors, recognized that the only way to help anybody was to help ourselves and be the model and guide for others to do the same. Doing anything less would simply contribute to the problem. Just imagine: if you are a part of a group of people being pulled down a river by a strong current and you want to help yourself and others, you must first get yourself out of the current, out of the river and onto the land. You must secure or fasten yourself to a stationary object and be stable and settled. Only then can you start to throw out life preservers to try to help others get out. If you have not secured and taken care of yourself, you are really no help to anyone else. By being the model, you can guide the way for another, and truly help. Anything less is simply contributing to the existing problem, or worse, creating new problems. Find your strength, be the model and truly contribute to the wellbeing of the rest of us.

We had to face all this ourselves and we understand the struggles, consequences and blessings associated with doing this. By fixing ourselves, which continues to this day, we naturally became the model which helped others to do the same.

Know that the only one you can change is yourself and you do have the power, within you, to do so. We all do. So if you are feeling continuously stuck you need to reexamine your belief systems and change the questions you are asking. Go to what you are feeling or believing and ask if it is really the truth.

Remember:
- Spells or beliefs are blockages that hold you back.
- Now that you are aware practice self-care, self-love, and self-respect.
- Throw out all that doesn't serve you.
- Choose not to live in illusions created by the drama of yourself and others.
- Decide to be courageous and pull yourself out of the equation.
- Don't take anything personally.
- Get out of your own way.
- Understand you are something more than just a 'me.'
- Get that you are perpetually in motion and a vibrating, moving energy.

- Know that movement is all around and within you, and therefore, so is change.

You are only stuck if you allow outside forces to interrupt your living, and if you refuse to embrace the motion of who you are. As English physicist and mathematician Isaac Newton's first law of inertia reminds us: every object in motion stays in motion until acted upon by an outside force. So when in the flow of movement You are not stuck, you are always part of the All, a very important part, yet a part. You are a moving part of something greater and what you say and do affects all those around you, and the rest of the All.

So:
- Analyze your vocabulary and toss out all negativity you tell yourself and the universe, about yourself and others.
- Remember that your words, speech and thoughts are powerful vibrational energy spreading out into the universe.
- Clearly emit good things for yourself, others and your environment without being caustic or redundant.
- Be aware of the clear and simple vibration of truth within you, move with it and be free.
- Don't underestimate what you are truly capable of doing and expressing, and joyfully embrace your own power and wisdom.
- Accept your insight, focus and meditate in that space.
- Minimize distractions, and be clear about your intention and questions.
- Understand that everything isn't all about you.
- Get that self-care is important, in your living and in the beliefs which structure your life.

Decide what to believe and allow this book to help guide you to answers within. By opening up this channel You now decide how You are going to show up for yourself in your life. Clean out what is not working for you and find energetic sustenance in the invocations you choose to experience.

What are Energetic Invocations?

If you take energy and you invoke it with your will and desires, you can create energetic invocations. They bring a change in perspective, a shift inside you and a cellular difference. They are moments of clarity, on steroids. As you feel energetic invocations, energy moves inside you. Our readers have shared that they experience lightheadedness, a somehow knowing, a warmth, and an overall peaceful feeling. And you will too, because energetic invocations heighten clarity and open the truth within you.

So, resonate with the vibrational charge of their energy and note how you change. Adopt each invocation for yourself, adapting it to what resonates for you and altering it for your specific intent. Allow each invocation to change your world as you see fit.

Change in your life is okay because change is life and having it in your life means you are living and are alive. It is productive and enhances your growth as you move through this work, so engage change with clarity and celebration, focusing on your intention. Others' intentions are not for you to follow. Build your own intentions and powerfully stand by them with vigor and gratitude. In doing so you find the path to change yourself and your world.

- For you are a part of the solution because you, with all of us, are a part of the problem.

Journeying deeper into your focus opens up new, creative solutions. With this book you can define yourself and your journey, investigate the people and environment around you and explore the world within which you live. Organized by sections and themes, **Energetic Invocations: A Book of Vibrational Change** helps you identify and reflect upon beliefs or spells that have become influences. By absorbing the words, feeling and energy as only you can, reflect and take time to process yourself. Then get involved in the powerful conversation, and join us, the authors, by experiencing ***The Energetic Invocations Audio Series.*** It includes the sections of the book along with invocations, read by us, and a special Authors Cut which divulges the origination of the process and the energetic background behind it.

In using this book, you will construct a map which will lead to your truths. Plot your course by actively defining your stuck beliefs, where they come from and how they are created. You are the traveler in your life journey and it is about time you played a major part.

Ask yourself:
- What is my blockage?

  Where are you stuck and what beliefs are holding you there?
- What is the origin?

  Where did this belief come from?

  Who did it come from? What did they do to make it appear real?
- How does it manifest in my life?

  How do you create everything that occurs because of this belief?

  When and where does it exhibit itself in your life and living?

With these questions you actively observe your actions, and take inventory of your behavior and life. Quantum Physicists say that when you look at something you change the way it behaves. The minute you interact with something there will be a reaction: good, bad, or indifferent. So, by acknowledging and observing your belief, you change your interaction with it: good, bad or indifferent. You either choose to adopt it (therefore it is good), you decide it is not your truth and remove it (therefore it is bad), or you realize that it is not all that important one way or another (indifferent). The difference is that you now have awareness of your thoughts and beliefs and how they impact your life, and you understand that there is a choice. The belief has changed. When you observe your beliefs, you look at them and are aware of them. Acknowledging the belief separate from you allows you to change it.

- So simply in finding your beliefs, and understanding where they come from, you have awareness of how they affect you and impact your life, and you have a choice whether to continue with them or not. It's that simple.

It is very possible to find your beliefs and let them go, with love and gratitude, but it is a significant process and it is the crux of the work in this book. Letting them go with love and gratitude requires that you understand the impact of the belief on your journey. Every situation and person, whether a negative or positive influence, had an important impact on your life. By understanding that, you can let go of the anger, frustration or grief that you have been holding on to and therefore let them go with love and gratitude.

Going to the core of your beliefs will change the way you behave and help you find your truth. In examining your beliefs, you release them, empty your space of all not serving you and bring yourself clearly into a new picture defined only by you, rather than by others' beliefs or perceptions. Be honest and powerfully do the work, moving forward with determination. You are important and do matter.

Realize that and allow this book to help focus your attention. It will not give you answers or do the work for you, but it will challenge you deeply so you must show up for yourself and ask the right questions. Doing the work does not mean reading the pages, it means doing the detailed, time consuming work to uncover your truth and power.

Read the invocations, make them your own and align with your power. The invocations invoke clear, natural, energetic vibrations that you create, manifest and control based upon your intent, focus and thought. These energetic invocations transmit healthy, positive energy for and around you. Science states that energy is exchanged between individuals and their environment via continuous electromagnetic radiation emanating from all of our atoms. In fact, according to Research Scientist Dr. Valerie V. Hunt, known for her pioneering work with bioenergy, this energy is one of the two primary electrical systems which exist in the physical body. The other system governs muscles, hormones and physical sensations and works with the alternating electrical current of the nervous system and the brain.

Expanding and organizing your energy by utilizing the Energetic Invocations as an activation tool may move you into healthy, inspiring spaces. Comfortably contemplate them in stillness and silence, allowing the words and vibration to resonate into your cells. Feel empowered to personalize each invocation however you see fit as they are only guidelines to help you start on your own journey. Remember that this is your work and your journey, and it is your business.

Truly walk your path and know that You are rooting for you. You are here, whole, complete and perfect just as you are. Believe that, understand that and make room for the truth. Focus on your travels, not your destination. Enjoy every step of your journey like you never have before because You have nothing to lose and everything to gain. All is possible without limitation. Have confidence and joy in your truth, maintain that awareness to take care of yourself and take nothing and no one for granted. You are your business and you are important. So do the work, clearly emit your intention, focus, learn, move and have an enriching, powerful life!

Part One - Self

Volume 1: Who I Am? *Worth*

Understanding who you are is an important part to understanding your life, what it is versus what you hoped it would be. Once you get to the truth of who you are, it may seem that the challenge is to live from that truth. But how could you not? Being all of who you are is why you are here, isn't it?

So, who do you believe you are? Who do you think you came here to be? Challenge yourself to really know who you are. The exercises within will help you with that but you *must*, absolutely *must*, know that you were never put here to be just like anybody else. You were meant to be you. The President was meant to be the person he is, Jack the businessman was meant to be Jack, and Mother Teresa was meant to be Mother Teresa. How about You? No one can answer who you were meant to be, except you, so know that you were meant to be nobody else on this earth but you.

So why do we try so hard to be like somebody else? We compare ourselves to another person and put judgments on how we are better than, or not as good as him or her. Competition and our ego were meant to help define each of us differently and help push ourselves to be our best selves. But instead, the spirit of the ego has been beaten down, and because of that we have lost our true sense of who we are and our individuality.

Ask yourself:
- What defines you?
- Where does your sense of self come from?
- Who determines your sense of self?
- How do others value and see you?
- How does all of the above affect how you value yourself?

All too often others tell you who you are and this sets your beliefs about yourself, much like a spell cast upon you. Others' beliefs do not benefit you. Can any belief that is not based in truth ever benefit you?

Process this:

Were you one of the many young men or women who grew up being told that being a good caregiver and putting everyone else's needs in front of your own made you a good person who would be rewarded by society? Society and the media emphasized that role by showcasing people who gave what they didn't have as well as highlighting those who rebelled and were "bad." Didn't this lead most to believe that there was only choice A or choice B? With just two roles to choose from, very clear verdicts create biased reputations based upon which role is chosen. Where does anyone get off deciding you fit into choice A or choice B? Isn't there another choice, other than those based upon other's beliefs?

So:
- Have you made a life of believing what is not based in fact?
- Are you afraid someone else is going to see the real truth about you?

Have you worked hard to fulfill others beliefs and succumb to their definitions? It is time to excavate your own truth, reevaluate once held beliefs and definitions and live from a new, healthier space. Once you do, your life and world will change.

By purging stuck beliefs, where they come from and how they were created, you start being true to yourself and traveling further along the road to remembering who you are. Review your childhood, parents, hometown, relationships, familial dysfunction and unfulfilled dreams and there you will find blockages waiting to be healed.

Ponder the following questions in meditation or with a qualified therapist to start investigating who you really are:

A.) Find messages and wisdom from the events in your childhood and ask:
- What was the true experience of my childhood?
- What and who was around me, what was I told and how did this affect me?
- What did I do and not do, create and 'make-believe,' and why?

<u>Process this:</u>

Even as a young child, were you brought to believe you were meant to be the caregiver, peacemaker, sacrificial lamb, or black sheep? Were you bullied until you succumbed to the group mentality? Did you do the bullying just to survive? Were you given the task of being the "enforcer" of the group? Look at what "roles" you played, whether you chose the role or whether it was given to you and see how it has played out in your life. For example, one patient realized as the oldest child she was forced to mediate fights between her mother and father. Her family established that it was her job to create peace, stability, and harmony, a hefty load for a child. Having learned and perfected that role, she was bullied into remaining the peacemaker and even found her career as a manager, doing the same in the corporate world. As an adult she finds this skill of fixing relationships vital. We support her in expanding this role, as it has brought her success as a manager. However, she is now aware of this and now chooses how and when she uses it. She is no longer interested in some of the limitations and demands it placed on her. She decides how and when she uses it. The bullied role of family mediator no longer applies to this patient. She was not required to discard all of the support and lessons she learned, she simply now chooses what she wants to do with them.

B.) Move into the now and ask:
- What parts of my life feel at peace?
- What parts of my life don't feel at peace?
- How did I develop and what stopped me or changed me from developing?
- So can I define who I am for myself and be content?

So, at this point, certain patterns should be emerging. This is when you need to be kind to yourself and hold back any judgment. Judgment towards yourself and others will only come in and cloud the process. This is all amazing information that you can use to move forward. If you start to get caught in the emotion, you need to let it process. Until you are clear of all emotions (anger, grief, shame, beating yourself up, etc.), you cannot move past it. In understanding it had an influence on you, and getting past the emotion, you can learn, move past it and grow from it.

<u>Process this:</u>

> When a student graduates from elementary school to middle school, s/he takes what was learned (Math, English, etc.) and builds upon it throughout the remaining school years. Arguments, disagreements, unfairness, favoritism by earlier teachers, adults, etc. happened and affected the student, but s/he needs to let it go to move on and learn new lessons, and deal with new situations. As adults, we don't have that same benefit of an ending school year, graduation, etc. to establish a moving on, but we still need to go through that process.

C.) Focus on the defining experiences in your life by asking:
- What lessons will help me to understand who I am?
- Who do I blame, and why am I cynical about what has occurred in my life and world?
- Do I label myself a victim and if so what do I believe and why?
- Have I courageously met experiences or do I choose guilt and remorse over gratitude?

If you question which experiences are the *defining* ones, the ones that come to you are those for you to review. This is the beginning of starting to trust what you get.

By honestly contemplating and working through all of these questions and embracing any others that come up, you are doing the work. Take the time to ask yourself any other questions which come to mind that may help you remember who you are. By doing this you are standing in a new place and having a conversation with your true self. You are accessing your voice and encouraging it to be clear and free. You are important, you are worth it and it is about time you started listening. This is not easy and at first might seem strange, but in time you will begin to understand more and it will come together. Stay with it and be honest with yourself.

For the only thing you have control over is yourself and the more you keep listening to your voice the more it reveals the truth of your soul and gives you the wisdom to make correct choices. When you are really accessing your voice you are in a different energy.

Process this:

The voice we are speaking of is not judgmental or comparative and doesn't get into details or story. It is more of a global, all-

encompassing voice. The only examples we can give are: in church, you hear it when you pray; in meditation, you feel it move through you. It is never definitive, yet it is a potent force.

Drawing from this source helps build self-confidence, self-care and greater trust. Finding your own unique selling point and genuine authenticity allows you to see the same in others which reminds you that we are all connected, as part of everything. By embracing your awareness and integrating it into your living you realize how truly valuable you are.

In turn, you become grounded in the fact that you are completely in charge of your own happiness, one which no one can take away.

<u>Process this:</u>

If you believe you are in charge, then you have to believe that no one can give happiness to you, or take it from you.

Acknowledging this helps you open to growth, change and self-care. By taking care of yourself and others, with your ego intact, you learn and find your special gifts, loves and uniqueness. The individual ego, which is a natural and important part of who you are, needs to be better understood and utilized in a newer, different way.

As a huge part of who you are, the ego:
- is your self-esteem, self-importance and sense of personal identity,
- houses your consciousness, according to Sigmund Freud, Austrian neurologist and founding father of psychoanalysis,
- helps you self-actualize into your full essence, exhibiting entelechy, which Aristotle described as a vital force that directs an organism to self-fulfillment,

- is the driving force which aids you to further understand and embrace what you do well while realizing what is challenging,
- distinguishes you from others allowing you to excel in different ways and revere genius while appreciating the similarities in DNA, and
- is blamed for generating today's self-centered population, often said to be lacking concern for others.

Process this:

If the ego is responsible for our self-preservation, why are we giving it such a bad reputation? Our ego highlights our strengths and weaknesses and makes us unique. Of course, a society that has a role for you will want to beat the ego down.

For as an energetic being you are always connected to the All, yet you still individually exist, and adjust and grow in the physical world of interaction. Your ego takes note of what you like and dislike, excel at and struggle with and what you would like more or less of in your life. If the ego is allowed to thrive, we are able to become strong, balanced, growing individuals. However, if the ego is abandoned, ignored or beaten down, by denying individuality in order to fit in, this could cause us to feel inadequate, shame or guilt, which attacks our self-esteem. Worse, if abusive situations force us into survival mode the ego may take refuge or go into overdrive and then we are seen as negatively valuing materialism and competition over others.

So whether the situation be painful or not, it is important to remember that the ego will always follow instructions to uphold self-preservation. As many cultures are inherently built upon obligation, and we become sensitive to even the smallest incidents, we create layers of automatic habitual responses laced in guilt. When responsibility and guilt are forcing the ego to deny its ability to individualize and it is forced to fit in, the ego questions what is occurring and how to escape. If the sense of purpose becomes warped the ego may disappear or take complete charge as it enters crisis mode and denies harmony. This all affects your ego's ability to acclimate you to the world and assist in your self-realization.

> To get the ego in line you have to:
> - get rid of guilt, obligation and unrealistic responsibility,
> - lead by example and not cause pain to yourself or others, and
> - not pretend to be something different and separate from another or forcibly try to get what you want or need by bullying.

Realizing this may help you understand your own actions and aid in your growth. Look at yourself and the people in your life to determine who is bullying you or if you are the bully.

> Bullying:
> - is manipulation most often disguising itself as survival,
> - does not only appear in schoolyards, but also offices, grocery stores, hospitals, and homes and behind the faces of mothers and fathers, sisters and brothers, friends and acquaintances and even doctors and teachers,
> - gives the illusion that what you need or want can only be obtained through force and intimidation,
> - may be recognized in oneself as well, for each of us has the potential to be a bully in one way or another, and
> - can be changed with understanding, awareness and effort.

Process this:

> Society believes to remedy bullying means chastising the bully. Isn't the real solution in empowering the ones who are being bullied? This is why the bullying problem is only getting worse in every layer of society. Until we change the focus of the solution, the bullying is not going to change.

You will always get what you need or want and do not have to pretend to be anything other than who you are. Only by empowering ourselves with skills and the self-confidence to express fears and strengths may bullying be addressed. Then, rather than fitting in and succumbing to society and social media mores, bullying so as not to be bullied, may finally disappear allowing the ego to do its job.

So embrace all parts of this book while understanding the important role of your ego. For an ego out of whack, prone to outbursts and manically acting as a survivor or a controller needs balance. So address it, utilize it, see it for what it is and be aware because it is not going to disappear and cannot be ignored or destroyed. Make it an essential tool in your reawakening of the importance of 'me' and 'I.'

For in its purest form, the balanced ego:
- helps you work towards your highest and best interests,
- self-actualizes and expresses your creativity and differences as you learn from yourself and the energies all around you,
- performs like a movie star flourishing under the guidance of a masterful director,
- gives you strength to follow your own intuition,
- helps you realize your purpose and fulfill your potential,
- guides you as you explore the physical manifestation of your experiences, and

- will help redefine you rather than threaten to run your life.

By realizing your ego is there to help, you push your reset button. As the ego assists you in developing your individuality, you unveil who you are naturally supposed to be as you conscientiously do the work to define who you are. So embrace experiences as lessons designed specifically for you.

Once you do that you don't have to repeat those kind of experiences anymore. Instead, your awareness elevates and change occurs. Understanding what awareness is, developing it and maintaining it is important.

Awareness:
- is true clarity,
- will resonate for you as a real vibrational truth, that provides understanding,
- puts you within your own power and sense of self as you move from story and extract yourself from other people's stories,
- helps you act rather than react, especially when others affect you or you try to fix them,
- is realizing that nothing is personal,
- enforces that truth is always in your highest and best interest and beliefs are subjective, and,
- challenges you to be awake to the people and elements surrounding you and all that occurs and doesn't.

<u>Process this:</u>

People ask what enlightenment is. We find awareness synonymous. It is like a truth serum. You see beyond what is being presented. You understand what real power is. And all stories become transparent. Nature seems louder to you. None of it is personal. Could you really live like that?

You are going to be challenged as you continue on with the exercises in this book, yet by simply acknowledging and having awareness you will create change. Where your attention goes your energy flows and your awareness can counteract the force of others' beliefs and incorrect definitions, energetically changing your growth and understanding. If you have awareness of what is going on and your part in and around it all, everything changes. Finding and being in that awareness is the true work.

Use the Energetic Invocations for *Who I Am?* as an activation tool to expand and organize your energy and move you into healthy, inspiring spaces. Comfortably contemplate them in stillness and silence, allowing the words and vibration to resonate into your cells. The invocations are guidelines to help you on your own journey so feel empowered to personalize them however you see fit.

<u>*Who I Am Invocations:*</u>

1. I am more than me.

2. I am a part of the grand scheme, in alignment with and in synchronization with its power.

3. Me is the individualization of the All and therefore no less important than the All.

4. I am the intention of my highest and best essence.

5. I am empowered and empowering within and without.

6. I am dynamic, essential and balanced in the realm of knowing.

7. I am a significant part of a significant and abundant All.

8. I am capable of creating any and all things of my choosing and am encouraged to do so, for the heart of our essence is to do nothing other than create.

9. I am energy. I am creating the Universe and the Universe flows through me and guides me.

Now you are aware, so be clear about who you are, what the truth is and where you are going in every moment. You are smart so work intelligently being honest and truthful with yourself. Don't be foolish or take things personally. Have the clarity to know what it is you want and operate from that intent. You make decisions for you and there is no story but truth. That is the real way to heal, to grow, to live.

If you think this first chapter has been challenging and you want to give up don't distress because as you peruse this book you will revisit this chapter and the others many, many times. It is a significant part of the process because it is for you. Embrace it and push through it. Work with it and change will occur within yourself, your environment and with how those around you see you. So don't be surprised if you are continuously triggered by those around who have helped you lose your sense of self in the past. The real challenge is remembering the truth of who you are and living from that very powerful place until it becomes habit.

Volume 2: How do I exhibit self-care? *Happiness*

- Who is the one person you can change? You.
- Are you looking outside to fix your problems?
- Are you looking for everyone else to change your world and make you happy?
- You change your world by changing yourself.

Process this:

True self-care benefits everyone. When you have mastered self-care you are happy. Once in that space, you will have validation. For, whoever fully resides in self-care wishes for everyone else to be there with them. You feel happy when good things happen to others. Jealousy, anger and resentment fall away.

In order to change, you have to do the work. Having constant awareness of your own self-care helps you do this. When you practice self-care you uncover the truth. You heal, learn and grow as you take care of yourself.

Self-care is not:
- being selfish, greedy, overindulging, competitive or judgmental,
- hurting yourself or others, or denying others,
- hoarding, squandering, or taking anything from anyone else,
- doing something out of guilt or manipulation because of someone else,
- having fairytale illusions of someone else taking care of you,
- fulfilling a definition of yourself because others have defined you that way,
- acting damaged, or as a martyr, desperate to help others, or
- taking things personally and falling into the drama of stories.

Process this:

> *Do you find yourself going the extra mile for everyone else? If you are always tired, restless, and overwhelmed, and available for everyone, you are not exhibiting self-care for yourself.*

Self-care is:
- celebrating your life and choosing to be mindfully present for yourself,
- remembering who you are every moment of every day,
- courageously inviting experiences for you to learn and grow from,
- being fully and completely present in each and every interaction,
- listening to your inner voice,
- actively making decisions that are best for you and respecting them,
- trusting and having confidence in the wisdom of your inner self, and acting and living from that truth, and
- becoming whole and sharing that completeness with your community.

When you express who you are, you act from your truth and trust the wisdom of yourself. Operating with awareness and being fully in the space of who you are helps you exhibit constant self-care. This same awareness and presence can be found in nature.

For both day and night, nature simply is and exhibits self-care by being what it is. Trees are, quite simply what they are and are present in their own existence. They grow, bear fruit, shed, provide shelter and die. All the while a tree is a tree and does not try to be the ocean or the sky. Nature gently and with intent, emerges, grows and evolves all the while exhibiting self-care. Yet it lives in harmony with all around. Once you put yourself into that energy you will practice self-care and live in that same harmony. The Chinese Yin and Yang symbol is the representation of this harmony.

Our physical and energetic presence is affected by our thoughts which help direct chi, our life force energy. We all carry within us the necessary energies to balance and heal. Yin and Yang help create this fluid balance. Where Yin is female, cold and nourishing chi, Yang is male, hot and protective chi. Yin and Yang carry the seed of opposites and flow in an alternating cycle. This flow, also expressed as the Tao, 'the Way,' balances the merging of impermanence with limitless yet cooperative existence. Being aware, attuned, informed and sensitive to this flow is part of self-care.

Unless you have visited and exhibited self-care, how would you be capable of giving to others freely and without expectation?

Process this:

> *If self-care is not a priority, then you are not truly helping anyone. If you give something that you are already lacking it is going to balance itself out in some way. As a practitioner, if you are worn out and tired and taking on all these patients you may feel like you are doing so much good and if self-care falls to the bottom of the list you think it is okay. But the truth is you are giving and giving so the taking is coming from someplace or someone; it is impossible to sustain giving when you are not receiving or practicing self-care. If you're not practicing self-care, somebody is feeling the brunt of it: a loved one, a roommate, or that unsuspecting patient that is not as needy as everyone else. So by dismissing self-care you are no different than the problem that you think you are fixing.*

If you have not satisfied your needs, how could you possibly give to others with the hopes of fulfilling someone else's needs? If you are giving what you don't have, that is an indication that you are not giving wholly, and without expectation. This does not relate to money, it relates to self-care. If you are lacking and you give, you are most likely looking for something in return if you are truly honest with yourself. Might you be looking to fulfill a belief that you have regarding worthiness? Are you expecting that this now makes you worthy? Do you believe you are now deserving of something in return?

Process this:

How many times a day do people take things believing they deserve them? Do you do this? If you do, then you must believe that you need to earn the right to exhibit self-care, and have money, abundance and a happy life. The idea of "deserve" is linked to a lack that you believe you need to make up for, when the truth is there is nothing you lack. What you are given is not because you deserve it. It is simply a birthright for being here and exhibiting self-care. When you think you "deserve" something, it infers you are taking it from someone else who doesn't "deserve" it. This isn't the truth and is wrong thinking. What you receive comes with no strings attached, not at anyone else's expense and not in lieu of someone else receiving the same.

Know that:
- 'Deserving' is based upon beliefs which create expectations and trap you in old ways. Arguing you deserve something is as damaging as convincing yourself of your unworthiness to have it.
- Choosing an item or person to fill a void is not self-care. It is an unfulfilling disguise that surrounds you with lack. If you are emphasizing that in your vocabulary you are setting yourself up for failure.
- Ultimately, lack of self-care creates a needy individual.

By believing you deserve something you limit yourself, so be smart and realize you do not deserve anything because you can have anything without the need of providing a reason or showing entitlement. Believe in yourself, remember who you are, and be present in your own decisions throughout events and interactions. If you are not doing this you are not exhibiting self-care. So change your reaction and keep your best interests in mind. The more powerful you become at exhibiting self-care the more your environment will change. Once you habitually incorporate extreme self-care into your life you will elevate its definition and step further into your own knowledge and awareness.

Use the Energetic Invocations for *How do I exhibit self-care?* as an activation tool to expand and organize your energy and move you into healthy, inspiring spaces. Comfortably contemplate them in stillness and silence, allowing the words and vibration to resonate into your cells. The invocations are guidelines to help you on your own journey so feel empowered to personalize them however you see fit.

How Do I Exhibit Self-Care Invocations:

1. *I experience the full expansion of Yin to Yang energy, so deeply within me, where I go outside of the box.*

2. *I have the clarity to know what it is I want and I operate from that.*

3. *I listen to the voice of my heart, my organs, etc. and honor them.*

4. *I allow myself the moment to consider what I want to do.*

5. *I stop considering everyone else's needs and actively participate in my own life.*

6. *I don't go where I am not invited.*

7. *I mind my own business, because nobody else is minding it, with care.*

8. *I do what I love without hesitation.*

9. I repeat until I believe, without pause: "I am whole, perfect, strong, powerful, in harmony, happy, healthy, beautiful and loved."

10. I acknowledge that I am a spirit and I am part of something greater. I remember who I am.

Volume 3: What is it like to be healthy?
Influence/Charity

How could charity be linked to being healthy? Read on.

Being healthy is not just looking good to feel better. It is communicating and responding to your body, mind and spirit as they interact energetically and physically. Taking your body, mind and spirit into consideration in unison, synchronization and individually is being healthy.

Outside of yourself, health care has been organized to both assist and often distract you from your ability to be responsible for your own activities related to healing and being healthy. At its core, health care is still people healing people but it is a business with medically trained professionals, office workers and highly paid executives, all in search of customers. Most often, office visits are on a predetermined schedule in association with statistics, rules, procedures and internal controls that presuppose your symptoms, experience, recuperation and treatment.

•As a patient, remind yourself:
I am a powerful, healthy, complete and whole being. At the center of everything, I can heal myself.

At times, things may become unbalanced and illness could arise. You might need help and asking for and receiving this help is ironically part of your journey. Not everyone who is sick is choosing sickness over health. The sickness referred to here is the one which is tied to not being in the truth. Once you can open to the truth of your sickness you are able to heal or move ahead with any illness or disability and still grasp your life with vigor and wholeness. Nothing is a mistake and you are perfect. There is a wonderful buffet of Western, Eastern and varied holistic practices that can help you, however, only you can heal you.

Somewhere along the way we have forgotten that we can heal ourselves. We simply need to remember, and believe. Western medicine can perform miracles, and complementary medicine is a great adjunct, but in all cases, both simply fix a symptom. The only true healing comes from ourselves.

Process this:

The placebo effect has been documented in every clinical trial from biological, psychological and physiological standpoints. What is the placebo effect? It represents the classical sugar pill, which creates miraculous effects, when prescribed in lieu of the actual medicine. It can have similar or better effects than what is being tested. Although it is a part of every clinical trial, no one has been able to figure out how it works. So, does just thinking that something will heal you actually work?

As a patient, ask yourself:
- If I am sick and I just want to feel better am I paying attention to what is best for me and am I awakening from bad habits?
- Am I respecting myself and taking care of myself first as I engage in examinations and procedures and am I influencing my own healthcare?
- Am I confidently asking questions about everything with the intention of extreme self-care for my body, mind and spirit?

It is not unrealistic to expect your case to be handled individually with regards to your specific circumstances, medical history or diagnostic prescription. As healing is a very personal experience, off handed comments and suggestions made by trusted professionals may change the whole course of events for the patient who is expecting a good level of care. With many diagnoses, tests are subjectively interpreted and prognosis is determined by others' statistics. There is potential for incorrect analysis, incomplete follow-ups and additional costly, yet unneeded procedures. The individual who chooses a path that is less traditional is frowned upon and bullied by society's description of what you must do. There are many stories of healings that occur miraculously, so make those your focus. Always seek a practitioner that supports and encourages your individual healing style without judgment.

When people already see you as sick, your confidence is replaced by substantial doubt, whereby even doctors will predict a negative outcome.

Process this:

If you have been designated as the sick person in the group, did you choose this role? In **Part 1: Who I Am** *of this series we wrote about roles given to individuals and the beliefs that kept them in those same roles. This may not be the situation in every case but it is certainly worth investigating to see if you fall into this. We came in contact with a recently diagnosed cancer patient and his sister. His sister was overwhelmed with keeping her brother's focus on being healthy. Once the sister refused to see her brother as being sick, and conveyed that message to him, and he started to see himself as not being sick, a wealth of opportunities opened up to him. How he goes about it and what he does is his journey but that limited view expanded. Just by changing his viewpoint, new options opened up to him.*

Any patient thrown into this emotional chaos would find it hard not to feel guilty and follow predetermined procedures. Unfortunately, when care is based upon business rather than health, or even other people's situations rather than your own unique, individual case, there are few choices when threatened by death unless you comply with treatment.

It is hard to focus on the future when you are receiving a death sentence for a routine examination. But again, it is a matter of self-care, remembering who you are and being present with the power of your thoughts, while exterminating any and all who affect your environment with their own beliefs. Be grateful when diagnosis is in your favor and share your gratitude by communicating your hope to others inflicted. Even science supports the benefit of projecting good energy, as shown in the following examples:

- Albert Einstein was quoted as saying that imagination is more important than knowledge because it embraces the entire world, and all there will ever be to know and understand. So wouldn't it follow that if we utilize our imagination to create intense healthy thoughts, and make that our constant partner, we could alter our situations?

- Science has informed us that thoughts are energy and that biologically, we all have cancer in our bodies, whether it be proven as a by-product of guilt, angst, remorse or a constriction of energy. Nevertheless, does this mean we create sickness and continue to create it unless we choose otherwise?

- Dr. Masaru Emoto, Japanese author and entrepreneur, claimed that by exposing water to positive and negative thoughts the crystals created beautiful and ugly formations, respectively. As a high percentage of the body is water, can't we also contemplate the effect of negative thoughts upon our own cells?

- Dr. Judith Orloff, psychiatrist and author, says that what you believe will program your neurochemicals. So are you allowing unhealthy thoughts to imprint within your energy and affect your chemistry, vibration and frequency?

Medical appointments with misleading diagnoses and inconclusive tests force you to make choices. If someone has a preconceived notion about your health that you do not agree with it is up to you to show up for yourself and counteract it.

Don't be the victim, instead:
- Responsibly view your own health and never mind how others are viewing it.
- Reflect on your situation, ask questions, be actively involved and surround yourself with encouraging and supportive friends and family.
- Ignore others' spells and beliefs, protect yourself from unwarranted suspicions and be aware when manipulation is overshadowing personal attention and treatment.
- Replace guilt, doubt and chaotic worry with strong belief and determination.
- Remember that medical offices, hospitals and drug companies define you as their customer.
- Never let anybody label you as a victim or tell you how it is going to be. Understand you are the most powerful weapon for or against yourself.
- Use medicine to your advantage by being clear about your role in the business of it all.

Process this:

> *A colleague underwent a routine mammogram and was told that she had an abnormality. The colleague felt she was fine. But the medical community discounted what she felt, and saw her as another statistic. After being bullied by the medical community and being reminded that she was the mother of three children and it could be breast cancer, her beliefs were shaken so she went for further tests. While on the table during the ultrasound, she went clearly to a space of knowing that she was fine, healthy, strong and free of any disease. The radiologist was called in during the ultrasound because "miraculously" nothing could be found.*

Complex in its interpretation, the concept of healing is vast. There are many resources concerning the physical, scientific and spiritual aspects of healing, whether it be through a Western, Eastern, hybrid or holistic approach.

If you have aches and pains, listen to your body to flesh out why and how they are appearing. They are not random. You must investigate what you currently believe and do in relation to what is occurring inside and outside of your body. Are you choosing to suffer with pain as punishment or are you celebrating your awareness by counteracting unhealthy beliefs? As nothing is haphazard, by going deeper into pain and opening a dialogue you understand more. Sure you can attribute certain pain to random physical exercise or exertion but when you keep asking questions you continuously interact with your body.

You may even find ways to heal or at least move ahead in your life with more clarity and understanding, when you see how interactions and situations affect you. Forced into new views, even people with cancer have been known to speak about how their situations changed their lives. When facing any major issue, health or otherwise, you are often forced to evaluate everything. This could move you into a fresher outlook and lease on life. If you approach every situation as if it is designed specifically for you, you invite a different point of view and a healthier way of living. Not only in your attitude but also in your stance.

Alternately, if you choose to make yourself an ultimate victim you do not move closer to healing. What doctor, mystic or energy healer could heal you when you adamantly hold onto your ailment? Take the time to honestly ask yourself:
- Is being sick a way of life for me and what would happen if I wasn't sick?
- How would my family, work and social interactions change without sickness?
- Am I connected to these experiences as part of my ailment? What would being healthy change in my beliefs and thoughts of myself and my relationships?

Process this:

> A patient came to us with knee pain. He had been to every specialist and alternative therapist and we were his last resort. He had had knee replacement surgery and since then had chronic knee pain of which nobody could find the origin. After the first treatment, he was pleasantly surprised to be pain free. He waited to make a follow up appointment but finally did. At his second treatment he was surprised yet again and began asking questions related to his lack of pain and why it was happening. The fact that we didn't talk about why he didn't have pain and focused instead on the benefits of being pain free irritated him and he left the office. Two days later he contacted us, cancelled his follow up appointment and said the treatments were not working. To him just the thought of life without pain was enough for him to invite the pain back.

If you find no connection to these aspects then make a plan to feel better. You can do it. If you do find connections, go back to a time before you were sick, remind yourself how you were and ask yourself what it would mean if you weren't sick anymore. Granted sickness finds us all at one time or another but by being aware of our role and actions we can either sink into it or swim out of it. Remember that curing symptoms is the business of medicine and consists of only treating disease and returning the body to a state before the illness occurred, regardless of underlying emotional causes that could resurrect the sickness. Healing is putting the body in a better state than before it got ill by addressing the root cause of the disease, pain and illness and clearing it.

Practitioners and medical professionals can both help and hurt with healing. Doctors may remove tumors, restart your heart and dissolve blockages, but what you do after that will either enhance it or undo all of it. By leaving your healing up to someone else, you are being irresponsible. Instead, be thankful that others are there to help and assist you but realize that the true healing is your job. By being smart in regards to your health you are showing up for yourself, creating a space for yourself to heal and are taking an active role in that healing.

For when someone is sick, it is natural to create a space for healing. Whether the sickness is from birth, trauma, self-infliction, or any other reasoning, genuine helping may involve listening, being there, taking care of things and sometimes acting as a practitioner. People with problems have to be viewed with compassion rather than judgment, fear or anger. Even Pope Francis said that authentic power is service so when we freely share our service for the enrichment of others we feel powerfully whole and may find ourselves in the arena of charity.

Giving from a place of abundance allows you to give freely, without attachment or expectation. Charities, when utilized and serviced from a space of fullness and abundance can be beneficial to both the giver and the receiver. However, a charitable organization is like many institutions, and its donors and recipients can become victims of a misaligned intention.

One can clearly see that when an individual or company donates or assists to make a statement, attract publicity or fulfill ulterior motives, the motivation to help corrupts the actual charity. When a service is offered to relieve emptiness or fill a void for an individual or a company that too corrupts the charity.

<u>Process this:</u>

When a major corporation pays its employees a minimal amount, and where its vendors are pushed to present the leanest profit and still make the deal, and its customers are left with sneaky, underhanded business practices where they are unable to fairly negotiate their contracts, clearly the corporation is benefitting. So when said corporation then makes massive donations to a charity, the charity that receives the donations is therefore attached with that corrupt energy. Instead of masking their deceit by charitable donations of millions, how much more good would come from their donations if they established fair business practices from the start and made less of a donation.

Charities:
- help individuals working through difficult situations,
- provide guidance and care, when functional, with the understanding that the individual needs to do the work to eventually stand independently,
- are similar to a helpful doctor or healer, who, like a boat, transports someone stuck on an island back to the mainland, and
- are a helping hand given from a place of abundance, requiring nothing in return.

If intentions to donate are anything other than those listed above, it may be that the motivation is to receive something in return, rather than just give. If you find that a donation is given from a place of need, it needs to be reexamined. There is a greater potential benefit in using that money or service to enhance self-care or the lives of the people around you. A dollar's worth of fair practices, kindness and self-care can go further than 10 million dollars in donations.

<u>Process this:</u>

A + B = C   That is what we believe, correct? Well:

$10 million in unfair practices + $5 million in unfair payments = $15 million in donations

ABSOLUTELY NOT.

Don't you find it ironic that some of the biggest charities in the world were spun out from unfair business practices and yet those charities continue long after the corporations that started them? It seems as though the energy is still working to balance the trade.

So if you want to be a good person who gives to charity or offers your time as a volunteer, yet you never feel you have done enough:
- reevaluate your reasons,
- question where you are volunteering, and
- ask why you are giving.

If you are exhausted and are giving from an already empty pot it is time to reevaluate. You must: be clear about your motivations, examine the environments you pursue, analyze your role as a volunteer, and question your support of charity work. For giving freely and genuinely with a full cup, and without desire of receiving something in return is true, healthy, beneficial giving that helps create a space of healing for those sick and in need.

Remembering who you are, along with constant self-care, helps you to be healthy. Body, mind, and spirit interact energetically and physically. As your physical being entertains its need of manifestation and experience, your energetic feels, integrating satisfaction, peace, harmony and truth while aware and present. Being healthy in body, mind and spirit comprises investigating how you care about your health, what you do to stay present and alive, your awareness and how it influences you, and how you share your healing or lack thereof with others and yourself.

Use the Energetic Invocations for *What is it like to be healthy?* as an activation tool to expand and organize your energy and move you into healthy, inspiring spaces. Comfortably contemplate them in stillness and silence, allowing the words and vibration to resonate into your cells. The invocations are guidelines to help you on your own journey so feel empowered to personalize them however you see fit.

What Is It Like To Be Healthy Invocations:

1. I am aware of the truth.

2. I allow my body to talk to me and to hear me clearly.

3. I surround my environment with positive reinforcements of the truth.

4. I allow myself to open up to all types of healing experiences, even those of which I may not be conscious.

5. I do not allow myself to be defined by a conceived disability.

6. I believe in my ability to heal.

Once you know the impact of your words and your thoughts on your health, you can no longer beat yourself up, nor can you beat others up with those words and thoughts. You cannot perpetuate this behavior because if you do, you are part of the bigger problem. Once you are aware of this, you cannot be unaware. So, if your actions remain unchanged, then your behavior reflects your intention.

Part Two – Journey

Volume 4: How do I choose to live my life?
Gratitude/Guilt

You are able to choose what you want and create how you live. Moving forward in your journey, you learn, grow and adjust to new experiences. Your journey encompasses your life and is all about energy, interactions and perspectives surrounding experiences. Within this there is no destination, except presence, so how do you get the most out of your journey, every minute and every second?

- Remember that your journey is completely, just for you.

When you were first born, you knew who you were and what you wanted to do, in general terms. Unfortunately, as judgments and beliefs were thrust upon you, your sense of self was lost as your worth and purpose fought to survive. Just by being here, it is your choice to trust and embrace what occurs, as your journey is a chain of experiences that are sacred and worth celebrating. You can choose to express your journey in every moment, because life is a succession of experiences and what you learn from them.

Process this:

You are here, by no mistake, for your own best interest. Embrace it and make the most of being here.

If you are busy making plans to fill up your calendar with to do's, life still happens, with or without you. If you are trying to overly prepare it is likely that your agenda will be tested, and flexibility will be your only security. By relinquishing control you glide into a magical journey of wonderful and often heart wrenching experiences which will help you learn about yourself, others and the world around you.

Process this:

> Do you really believe you can control anything? The truth is that control simply limits you. Controlling something sets up limitations you are stuck with. You control nothing.

Yet no matter the situation, you may always ask yourself how to put the experiences of your life to good use, without doubting or qualifying them.

You can:
- share in the total experience rather than the drama;
- create experience by being in every moment, feeling your feelings and letting them go;
- stop repeating frustrating reactions, activities and to do's;
- dive into the truth of the matter, and disregard the story; and,
- realize that sometimes it is just about someone else and you need only be present and listen, and that might be all it is about, in relation to you.

Often people intercede in our experiences by pushing for what they want because they deem it to be in our best interests, even though it may have nothing to do with what we want. Then, misleading ourselves, we spend hours trying to make everyone happy. Sometimes we even put our lives on hold, figuring that once everyone else is happy, only then can we be happy. But by only making ourselves happy, and by being the model, can we then do for others.

Process this:

> If you are making others happy, could that be a stall tactic to delay your life? Who does it really benefit? It doesn't benefit you or the person whose life you are trying to run. Admit it, it's much easier to run

everyone else's life and squawk about how your own doesn't have your time for attention. If that's your truth, it's time to live your life.

What you put out is truly what you get back so:
- choose to investigate your own journey,
- change your perspective and your reactions and choose to mindfully live your life,
- be grateful that you are taking the steps to change your view of your life and understand it because it is your life, and
- choose to live it and experience it for yourself, rather than defend it to anyone else.

We defend ourselves often. We provide reasons and answers for everyone else, rather than the truth for ourselves. Whatever we are defending ourselves against actually has nothing to do with us. Most often it is a story, a judgment or an observation that attempts to control us or take our power.

Process this:

A friend shared that her sister-in-law's conversations are always defensive, full of reasons and stories of why she has to do what she does or feel the way she feels. Most often the conversations are one-sided with a lot of drama and convincing. But who does she think is listening? Instead of having a fun conversation, the sister-in-law ends up helplessly controlled by her story, in an endless cycle of struggle and defense. Sadly, some people live their entire lives defending themselves, constantly reiterating the same story to everyone. Yet who are they really trying to convince? Because most often, when a person does this others tend to tune out the story and not care. After all, which would you choose: a recycled, one-sided story that justifies someone's choices and beliefs, or an enjoyable, heartfelt conversation of which you are a part?

When you make something personal, you put yourself into a fight with yourself. How could you ever win against yourself? You cannot, so, you remain divided, living your life out for others instead of enjoying your own journey.

- For the moment you take something personally, your mind is distracted by unhealthy thoughts and it removes itself from its connection with the greater universe. Thus, your journey and your spiritual growth halts.

<u>Process this:</u>

Have you ever had a horrible retail experience where the sales clerk was so nasty that you ended up defending your request or walking out angry, upset and feeling like you got ripped off, all because you took it personally? Some people are going to have the same disposition, regardless of what you look like, say, believe or what nationality you are. Don't ask why they were mean to you. Many are not discriminating against you or any group, as they hate everyone. That clerk may be one of those people, so why are you wasting your time taking that personally?

By taking nothing personally, you realize the situation, story and participants are all there for a lesson. The experiences are an opportunity to learn and grow if you can grab a hold of that with intention. You can choose to walk that path or not, just as the participants around you can choose to or not. You have a journey just as they do, and somehow, it is all connected.

Yet, it is not for you to fix or judge others. If you interfere in others' lessons, they will have to go through them all over again until they figure them out. You are here to work, process and learn your lessons. And in learning and growing, you can have gratitude, for the experience, opportunity, other participants and the journey. Having gratitude allows you to move ahead in your life without guilt.

Process this:

> Focus on the word "fix." You can fix a plumbing problem, you can fix your hair, you can fix a meal, but can you really fix a person? You can't. You may think you are fixing him and his problems but you are really not helping him. Until he figures out how to fix his own problems, those same problems will keep coming back to haunt him. In fact, you both may become resentful, as he becomes dependent. We all know of someone who everyone thinks: "How is he going to survive after his mother, father or caregiver goes? That caregiver does everything for him." Yet, to everyone's surprise, when the caregiver is gone and he has to deal with his problems, he moves on quite well. If only the caregiver realized this was possible earlier on, dependency wouldn't have occurred, he would have worked through his problems, and their relationship would have been much richer.

- Deciding on what you *must* do moves you from the obligation, expectation and guilt of what you think you have to do. When you live from this, interactions become clearer, allowing you to open up to deep feelings of love and care in your heart.

As attachments are made to what is expected of us, or what we put upon ourselves, and whether or not we fulfill those expectations, we become addicted and are judged as successes or failures. If what we are doing does not serve our 'musts,' then we are existing from should, need, expectation and obligation, and are experiencing the pain and suffering of guilt. Guilt is a tool, which, like the ego, is misunderstood and is a bit out of control. The focus of guilt might have been to help us learn lessons, so as not to redo them. Its sister feeling, shame, helped to remind us not to do the same sequence of events that led to that 'shameful offence.' Shame and guilt are strong reminders of what we should not repeat. This feeling of shame and guilt and what it was supposed to invoke has been hijacked, and its purpose has been misconstrued. It has moved us away from what we must do to what we believe we 'should' do.

Today we know, as stated in Michio Kaku's, <u>*The Future of the Mind*</u>, there are three main parts of the brain. Our brain has evolved from a primate functioning brain to a more developed level, whereby it has learned to process a past and see a future. Kaku further relates the brains functioning within a three leveled space-time theory of consciousness. The first two levels of consciousness are unable to process time and exist solely in survivor function. The first level reacts to basic functions for survival. The second level utilizes the present space along with developed social skills. The human brain merges all of these while relying upon emotions to analyze and evaluate information, run simulations to reflect on possibilities and then make decisions. In doing so, we developed certain emotions and feelings to adjust to this new level of consciousness. Science has proven that we have evolved as a species and enhanced our abilities to discern patterns and look and plan for the future. Yet, weren't the emotions of guilt and shame available to help us learn what not to do in the future, based upon our past events? For then, they would aid in our decision making process, as they helped us learn and grow.

<u>Process this:</u>

Every day you run a lot of simulations to evaluate possibilities and make decisions. Guilt and shame help you to make the best decisions to fulfill a goal however you were not meant to sit and dwell in guilt, or shame. Similarly, a hammer was designed to help build magnificent buildings, not to hit someone on the head. We use hammers for many things today which are not its intended purpose. Is that how guilt and shame are being used today?

By focusing on what you must do rather than always providing for others, with guilt, you let others freely be around you. In turn, you shift from constantly nurturing others to modeling your freedom and theirs. Your gratitude can finally manifest receiving and create a heartfelt balance.

The more you practice being in gratitude the more you create an automatic habit, one that not only conquers guilt but is much healthier than guilt. For by moving from guilt to gratitude, appreciation comes.

- *Live in true gratitude, not other people's gratitude of you.*

If you choose not to live through expectation and obligation then you live purely through spirit. So many people use others as a tool to do their dirty work, and create illusions of tasks and obligations that others choose to do just to get them done. Never mind existing from doing things just to get them done, instead prioritize every situation for what it is and hold others accountable to responsibly act on their own behalf. If you do not do this, you will attract energies that will distract you from your own journey and dysfunctionally force you to prove yourself in a way that is not consistent with your own truth. When your energy and presence is required to settle someone else's journey, you can become subject to others' manipulations, perceptions, fears, understandings, judgments or controlling conditions.

There are times during our journey where life becomes so uncertain and we question where we are and what we are doing. It is during these times that we must understand we are only allowed to be certain of where we are or where we are going.

Process this:

You, the reader, are a part of it at this very moment. We, the authors are experiencing these very feelings. As much as we feel very passionate about what we are sharing and writing, we know that there are critics out there that will have opinions. This is an unknown territory for us. But we know how passionate we feel. We don't know where this will take us, yet we are inspired to go on as this is helping us and we believe this will help many people. We are, as you read this, in complete uncertainty as to where we are going. We are enjoying this process, where we are at this moment, and are staying focused on the energy.

Buddhists and Taoists remind us to be comfortable with this uncertainty. Science also supports this with the Heisenberg Uncertainty Principal. Werner Heisenberg, a German theoretical physicist and an originator of quantum mechanics, stated that the more certain we are of where a particle is, the less certain we are of where it is heading.

So how do you move forward with that principle in mind? You can only be certain of one thing, either where you are or where you are going. Know where you are, by knowing who you are. Where you go should not be defined by obligation or expectation.

Process this:

If you are troubled by your future, can you focus on what is going on now? Focusing on both is not multi-tasking. Focusing on your here and now means you can expressly direct your attention to what is going on and what you need to do, right here and right now. If you focus on your future, you are not here. You cannot be in two places at once, can you?

Discard all notions of burdens. Create a new space to access a higher vibration of all that will benefit you. Put your 'must do's' into motion with clear intent, be open to what comes your way. Remember that one person is not meant to do it all alone so you must allow things to get done by others. Be a model for those around you by taking it upon yourself as an individual to evolve with gratitude and without blame, specifically right where you are.

Perhaps it is a better decision to be certain of where and how you are here and now, rather than worrying about somewhere down the road that hasn't even occurred yet.

After all: Where you are, you are all of You, so be brilliant, present and fearless.

Life is cyclical yet you must remember that you are powerful and infinite. Everything changes and grows and you are a part of that process as well. Without limitation, you can do anything all along your journey.

That is the trip you have created for yourself. Be good with what you have done, live up to how amazing you are and do not waste any more time taking anything personally. Understanding this is the only truth that walks with you, and all those who truly walk beside you exhibit it, as well. It is an understanding that comes with living life and gaining strength from experiences, and it helps you to find wonder, embrace all that happens, and move beyond. That is your journey.

Use the Energetic Invocations for *How do I choose to live my life?* as an activation tool to expand and organize your energy and move you into healthy, inspiring spaces. Comfortably contemplate them in stillness and silence, allowing the words and vibration to resonate into your cells. The invocations are guidelines to help you on your own journey so feel empowered to personalize them however you see fit.

How Do I Choose To Live My Life Invocations:

1. This journey was created by me and is just for me.

2. Others' intentions are not for me to follow.

3. As I peel away 'old beliefs,' influences and ideas, the 'who I am' evolves and I will know who I am.

4. I am open to making drastic changes. I am open to all possibilities. As I remain open, I am ready to embrace abundance.

5. *The journey is a constant absorption of the daily magnificence, for my senses.*

6. *My journey is filled with plenty of vibrant causes that teach me to act and react, in ways that fill my presence.*

7. *I am capable of doing things in a physical form that are not possible in the pure energetic form. Therefore, the fact that I am here is significance enough. There is no 'to do.'*

8. *This is my journey. I have gratitude that its design is just for me and I embrace it.*

Volume 5: What can I create with my expertise?
Patterns

- What is expertise and where can you find it?
- Is your expertise your occupation or is it related to your money-making capabilities?

Expertise does not mean occupation. But expertise will follow you into your work. If you are very good with computers, you do not have to work in the Information Technology department of a company because you can use your skills and expertise with computers anywhere or in any field for business or for pleasure.

Expertise is not your money making capabilities, but it is what you like to do. If you are a Mathematician you probably have an affinity for symbols and money; a Chemist, for elements and equations; a Baker, for herbs and recipes; an Author, for words and stories; and a Musician, for sound and notes. Likewise, if you studied Reiki or Acupuncture, enjoy practicing and are talented at it, but do not have an office, you still have expertise. You can exhibit it by moving Chi, fleshing out blockages, energizing environments and even transforming workspaces. How you define it is up to you, because it is about what you like to do. Your expertise shows up and only you decide how to take it into your world, regardless of the money.

Your expertise is in your movement, in your expression and in the way you flex your mind and your muscles. Your expertise is in the structure of your thoughts, in the vibration of your senses and in the pulse of every experience that you embrace, encourage, and emit. Your expertise is in your everyday pattern of energy, how you see things, how you choose to perceive the world, how you live. It is your unique selling point, your moving energy, your immense power that is clear and true.

Your expertise is a gift, as well, for you to open, play with, explore, assemble and recreate. It is for you to share or not to share, in the way you decide. It is not about following other people's structures, beliefs or patterns or copying what others have done before. It is about acting presently in the comfort of your expertise as it moves through you and moves the environment around you.

Process this:

Expertise can be a hard concept to understand at first. It's easy when it's something that reveals itself so naturally and explicitly, such as an artist, musician, inventor, genius. Most of us are not so fortunate to be able to name the expertise so clearly. You might get a subtle hint of it, and it will evolve over time and may present more clearly in your future, or not. It will grow and expand as you do, or sit in the back quietly if you decide not to express it, however suppressing it will frustrate you. Most of the time you know it, and you might be embarrassed to admit it, or deny it, but you are aware of it. Simply making an effort to explore it, might give you the push that's needed to find it. At the very least, you now have awareness to seek it out whereby you might not have had it before.

Living, surrounded by and emanating your expertise is important to create, change, and move your world. It takes a huge leap of faith and courage to even acknowledge your expertise. Unfortunately, others may judge you if your expertise does not align with their beliefs of how you must utilize it. Their strategies may be relentless or hidden, but all the while, you must have conviction for who you are and what you can create with your expertise.

Your expertise may also change, adapt or recreate itself. If you are amazing with words and stories, as a Writer, you could easily turn into a Chemist and be just as incredible with molecules and matter. Likewise, a Teacher may transform into a Doctor, an Accountant into an Acupuncturist or a Carpenter into an Actor. It is a part of your journey to change, to wear different hats and to have many experiences because your expertise underlies everything you do. Your expertise is a part of you, but does not become the label of your occupation.

- What if you are more than what you think you are?

The truth is that you are more than what others have defined you to be. So, if you are struggling in an environment that portrays everyone else's definition of what your occupation or lifestyle is then it is time for you to show up for yourself and your expertise, by:
- operating in different parameters and patterns,
- flipping traditional definitions in outrageous ways,
- philosophizing, reflecting and regretting nothing, and,
- creating something, anything, everything, which nobody has thought of or attempted before.

Process this:

Taking the time to understand who you are, your expertise, and what you like to do is important, it is self-care. As doing this takes courage, others may be very uncomfortable with you doing something that they do not have the courage to do and might try to laugh or minimize this very important process. You might be judged but you will know the truth behind it. Keep the course.

Construct a definition that works for you and vocabulary that goes along with it, to support and empower you. Focusing on your expertise makes you alive and that energy will spread itself to others. But you do not need to verbally reveal or discuss your expertise, unless you wish to. You live your expertise and it is a part of you. It may be a part of what you do but it is not all and in some instances it may never be what you do, or how you are defined by others.

In searching for your expertise, you should begin by examining the one thing about yourself that you would change, if you could. Usually, that one thing that makes you different, that calls attention to you, that takes away your privacy and space, is the one thing you want to change.

Perhaps:
- You are easily moved to tears because you empathize with others?
- You attract strangers who think they know you and then want to converse?
- You creatively fix items or solve issues, which seem to stump everyone else?
- You draw profitable situations to yourself but only find yourself surrounded by victims?

If these kind of frustrating scenarios distract you from being who you are and doing what you want to do, then you have found where your expertise lies. If you are a gifted musician, artist, chef, etc., it is a bit easier to find your expertise.

Process this:

> *A woman worked in an administrative position, in a company where everyone was very serious and lightheartedness was frowned upon. This woman was what others considered a bit eccentric. She wore 1920's flapper clothing, very colorful outfits and bright pink feathered boas. She would roam the halls and find closed conference rooms with windows and meetings going on. She would stick out her tongue and make faces at certain individuals and laugh on her way back to her desk, where she had 5 screens of social media open. Her antics were not appreciated, especially by her direct boss. She was harmless and fun spirited. She added levity to the work environment and actually performed well until she started to get reprimanded. Once the reprimands got so overwhelming to her, she started having health issues. One could say her expertise got her into trouble, and she probably wished she could be just like everyone else, but as your expertise will, it shines regardless. Once you find your expertise, you must look for, or create an environment where it and you will be appreciated.*

Once you pinpoint attributes that define you differently, you unveil expertise and abilities unique to you. Being open to your expertise leads you to experiences. So do not allow others to confuse you or inappropriately define or interrupt the natural progression of your expertise. Do not copy others or get caught up in what you are told or are influenced by. Instead, go with what feels correct, what you truly like to do, and how you can express that in your life.

You may still feel puzzled by what your expertise is. In its naturalness it will show up anyways and lead you to enriching environments and opportunities. Just as an Autistic child impressively swims through his environment making connections and associations in unique, creative ways, the different will reveal itself as a gift. Temple Grandin, Professor, Doctor of Animal Science, and Autism Activist, naturally fabricated visual thinking, and it became part of her communication expertise as she integrated more with society. In turn, she has noted that future autistic minds may focus their expertise into amazing inventions, as long as they are not hindered by society's expectations.

So, your expertise is a part of you but not your definition. It encompasses you on your journey and expands and elevates you amidst points along the way. It is possible to even create illusions around and with your expertise, enhancing the space between where the physical and energetic work together. Your expertise is one astounding piece of you showing up.

Use the Energetic Invocations for *What can I create with my expertise?* as an activation tool to expand and organize your energy and move you into healthy, inspiring spaces. Comfortably contemplate them in stillness and silence, allowing the words and vibration to resonate into your cells. The invocations are guidelines to help you on your own journey so feel empowered to personalize them however you see fit.

What Can I Create With My Expertise Invocations:

1. I am in the space of my whole complete self that is there for me, all of me.

2. I define the expression of my true nature.

3. I allow my experiences to properly reflect who I am.

4. I recognize that I continue to be more than I am or can imagine myself to be.

5. I am in the space where the highest and best use of my expertise is for the good of myself and others and where it is most beneficial and appreciated.

6. By opening up myself to others' experiences, I am able to better define my expertise.

7. I ask that my reflection be true and clear of judgment.

8. My expertise creates my world, all the while my world is not defined by my expertise.

Volume 6: What is my currency?   *Essence*

•Is it how much money I have in the bank?

Your real currency is more than society's definition. Today, your value is based almost exclusively upon your net worth or what you have that others may want. In order to understand your real currency you must first define your value.

•How do you value yourself?
•What do you believe you must do to increase your value?
•Do you allow others to define your value for you?

Most people clearly value themselves based upon money: what they have, what they are worth, what they are making and what money is coming to them. That is their currency and how they base their interactions and exchanges, especially in business.

Process this:

In today's corporate world we are inundated with those who live bonus to bonus, paycheck to paycheck and miserly counting their pennies in the bank. We too thought that was an old Scrooge tale but we learned that the Ghost of Christmas future is alive and well in big corporations. That ghost survives on cash being king of the kingdom. Hopping from venue to venue, the bonus becomes the silver nugget of fortune. How unfortunate it is that in this instance, money is the only currency that is considered.

But, currency is not just about money.

Others may value themselves based upon how much they do for another. If they can fix everything, volunteer, and/or give of themselves, they believe they have more value. They may even feel guilty for not doing enough to enhance their value. Under these circumstances, they do things or acquire items so others will find them valuable. And in doing so, they create an endless cycle. These people who are looking for validation of their value from an external source do not understand that these sources are busy trying to enhance their own value. These external sources cannot see beyond their own need for validation. Those who look for validation from others, unaware that they will never receive it, are left feeling they have no value or currency.

<u>Process this:</u>

> We all have met people who live and operate thinking they have no value. They consistently try to prove something to themselves and everyone else over and over again. Where do you think this comes from? We believe that many of these issues arise from the lack of self-knowledge and not doing the work that we are imploring you to do. Instead, believing they themselves have no power, these people run from guru to guru believing someone else has the power to fix them. They do good deeds so someone will notice them. However they don't realize that no one is going to fulfill the void they have for themselves. Doing the work within this book helps fill this void.

•How do you define your currency?

This is not a difficult task if you remain open to new definitions. As an example, if you are a Graphic Artist you could define your currency in the following way:
- •What is of value to me and what makes it of value?
  Focusing on creativity and projects that inspire and challenge me. The freedom and sense of exhilaration that come from developing something and journeying into new artistic arenas.
- •Why is it important to me?
  I love being in the realm of design and enjoy meeting with other designers.
- •How does it relate to what others value?

Clients value the work I do when it satisfies their goals.
- How do I value myself and how do others value me?

I value my talent by using my skills in places that empower me. Others have said they value my reliability and creativity.
- So, how would I describe my currency?

My currency is related to the time, space, freedom, creativity and inspiration that surrounds my compensation, which satisfy my efforts. It is about more than just money. I value other people that find these just as important.

From a Graphic Artist's viewpoint above, a definition of currency includes focusing on searching for individuals who value themselves in the same way.

Process this:

> That you have a valuable currency can be a hard concept to understand at first. But it is not a difficult task if you remain open to new definitions. Defining your currency is to understand that it is more than money, and if you can get that, it is a great place to begin!

Money is not greater than the universe or yourself. So understand the real, undeniable value of you: it is your entire presence. Understand this, because you are unique, your journey is unique, your skill set is unique and your expertise is unique. There is no other like you.

The interactions we have, the causes we support and the events we attend help us define what motivates us and allows us to realize all that we are. They do not define our worth. They help define what makes one person an amazing athlete and another, a talented artist, or how others are wonderful at working with people, animals, others in crisis or just beautifying places.

Process this:

>The different interactions we have, each day, help us better define our expertise and our currency. We all have life experiences and events, challenges and different people with whom we interact. All of these provide rich experiences in which we are able to see what we excel at, don't do so well at, what we like and don't like, and what we want more of and less of. If we use these experiences for the purpose of analyzing those ideals, we can enrich our life. If we choose to get caught up in vindictiveness, anger, grief, revenge etc. and just focus on the story we lose that other valuable information, and life becomes stuck.

For example, in *"The Wizard of Oz,"* Dorothy traveled down the path of the yellow brick road, which allowed her to meet others, some who traveled the same path, who helped, encouraged and supported her. Some caused her pain and challenges, which presented her ways in which she, and her companions could learn and grow. Each character was on his own journey, searching out his individual goal. Each one had his own unique talents that contributed to the greater good of the group, which each discovered during this journey. In the end, the group realized that all that they searched for, Dorothy's ability to go home, the scarecrow's quest for a brain, the tin man a heart, and the lion courage, was always within them. Their journey led them to learn this lesson, and they found what they needed, but in the end, it was with them all the time.

Your value is a part of you. It is not something you must earn or request from another. If you look for outside validation, then you embark on an endless journey. For the one who believes that recognition from others, material items, or even just money shows their worth, has sold themselves short.

Your currency:
•comes from your essence, strengths and weaknesses,

- is affected by both the supportive and constructive influences of your background,
- relates to both skills you acquire and seem to be gifted with, and
- is what you offer for exchange.

Process this:

If you disagree, then how would you define yourself or your currency without these parameters?

How do you place a value on your currency in an exchange? Most people simply think of cash. What are other considerations you should evaluate?

- Space – the room and area that works for you,
- Energy – an empowering environment,
- Respect – valued acknowledgement for your efforts and skills,
- Time – what you do and how long it takes, and the balance with the weight of your exchange.

Allow yourself to receive what matches all that is important to you. Again, if it is only money, then you will have to learn to negotiate for a rate that pleases you. If you are willing to receive other considerations, then you must be aware of negotiating for those, in order to maintain your currency and have your transaction valued. Keep in mind, in every interaction there is an exchange in energy and a potential enhancement of vibration that must be valued.

With this new understanding, others might criticize you, telling you that you settled, gave up on your dreams, or even missed the chance of a lifetime. If your choices were made with clear intention, only you know the real truth, and that is all that matters.

Process this:

> Others may criticize you because of what you decide your currency is. Many people switch careers and people question that. One woman, for example, decided to go to culinary school, even though people thought she was crazy. As an MBA executive, she was making three times more than she could as a chef. She got something out of culinary school that deeply affected her. She didn't go for the simple fact of making more money. Others go to school because it increases their money making capability, and there is nothing wrong with that. Sometimes you make a decision to follow your heart and what you receive is much more than a monetary enhancement. Many people have lost money on get rich quick deals, as others invest in something they absolutely believe in, or in themselves for what they love, and there is never regret. The currency of who they are has been fulfilled.

But, if you feel you made a mistake, by misjudging someone else's valuation of you, what then? Does that mean that you overvalued or worse, devalued yourself? No, take it as a lesson to move forward. If the transaction does not honor your value, remove yourself from the relationship. If it is too late and you find you gave away your commodity under someone else's terms, rather than what was agreed upon, reevaluate any further transactions, and:
- allow yourself time to get angry, but do not fester in the drama,
- focus on learning the lesson and moving on, rather than berating and blaming yourself for how the transaction became corrupt, and
- process what occurred for no more than one hour, but enough time to regain calm and balance, otherwise the situation may snowball, forcing you to look for others to compensate for your loss.

Process this:

> A contractor signs a contract to do work and within the contract it states a bonus of some amount along with the outline of work to be performed. The contractor performs all of the work and expects to be

paid for the work, along with the promised bonus. But, the other party changes the expectation and now decides that the bonus will be paid after additional work is done. The contractor has many choices. Let's focus on the two extreme ones: Choice A is for him to get disgusted, forego any bonus and not finish the work. Choice B is for him to finish the work and get his bonus at the end of this new period. His decision should be what is best for him, not a reaction to prove any point. He may decide to stay on because it is satisfying a financial or other need. By making this choice, he in no way accepts any devaluation of his currency, as one might feel. As he finishes his work, he may choose to look for other contracts, work with another company, or discuss the incident with the other party, again, whatever is in his best interests. In doing what benefits him, he is staying true to his currency and continuing to value it.

As hard as it sounds, when you find yourself in this situation, understand that it is a lesson. Learn the lesson and move forward. Do not hold onto the disappointment or anger. If someone devalues you, you have awareness of it so remove yourself from it. You chose you, and succeeded in self-care. Removing yourself, does not mean fighting or seeking revenge, or walking off a job or causing harm. It simply means that you didn't allow them to devalue you, because you saw through what they were trying to do, so they did not succeed. Now, you know your value. You know who you are. In time, everything comes full circle and those who devalue others often end up in their own unhappy, unfulfilled space. Nevertheless, you cannot do anything other than take care of yourself.

- *Know your value, and only allow others who value you in the same way into your space.*
- *Your currency is just as important as everyone else's.*
- *Remember, life is not just about work.*
- *We are part of a greater force, and no one is more or less important.*

Process this:

> If someone does not live up to an offer promised, that is not a time to react in a violent or uncaring way to yourself or others. You need to decide what it is you need to do, while remembering that you determine your value. If you realize that you are accepting this situation because you need the money that is smart. Be clear that you are allowing it to satisfy an immediate need. You do the work with integrity and along the way you figure out another place to work, another contract to fulfill, or another situation where you are not devalued. The boss, or other people around you might make you feel like you are accepting this devaluation, but you will know the truth of the matter. With such clarity you will be able to better understand what else you might learn or gain from the situation. It is not a defeat so do not fall into disappointment and anger. If you do, then by default you are accepting that you are not worth your true value. As you continue to work your best, you will find an opportunity to value yourself appropriately. The choice is yours, never the other person's.

Again, we can be guided by nature. Worker bees in a hive, working as a team, perform specific jobs and duties to ensure their hive environment and their queen survive. They clean out the hive, tend to the queen, produce beeswax, forage for pollen, support fellow bees and are compensated within the bigger picture of a successful hive. By focusing on the big picture, you too can find a grander compensation that matches your desired environment.

Process this:

> Many times, people are in a position whereby they need to accept a job that they might feel is below them. Pay rate, benefits etc. might be less than they are used to. If the focus is solely on the pay, they might be missing the bigger picture. Suppose a writer takes a job at a fish market for $10 an hour, has she decided that that is really what she is worth? No, her currency changed, and this new venue will provide a new and creative outlet to add to her stories. She is not there for the money; she is there for something else. Her currency and its definition have changed. She should not beat herself up over that. Long ago, we met a man who

worked as a custodian at a local college. Every day he collected trash and vacuumed floors. His colleagues never suspected that he was an award winning pastry chef in Brazil. He was happy to work at the local university and have his children attend college for free. His currency changed. This job never implied that he was worth less than before. He knew what it meant to have his children attend school, so he was happy to do what he could for that benefit. If you know you can do a certain thing and you settle for a job where you are not getting paid what you are worth, it may just be a temporary thing. Remember, what you want is your currency, and your currency has changed for the moment. Don't beat yourself up. Do what is best for you for the moment and move forward.

Yet if you value your self-worth with only a dollar figure, the result is an insatiable situation whereby greed is never fulfilled. Your worth becomes tied to what you get financially, which becomes an unending void, much like a shopaholic who just shops to satisfy an addiction rather than for any need. Valuing yourself on someone else's dollar, rather than how you truly value yourself, pulls you away from your truth. You are devalued when assigned a dollar figure that is not your currency. Not only is the devaluation a reflection of the person valuing you, but it also reflects his judgment of you.

You must have the courage to trust yourself and honor your currency. Your currency aligns with your essence, all you are, what you are trying to do and how you are trying to live. The opinions and judgments of others are not important, but understanding your currency and those of the people you are interacting with is vital. Communications and negotiations enhance when you operate from truth. No matter the cost, you must honor your currency, or no one else will.

Be clear of your value and focus on making your currency as valuable as possible. If your focus is on doing your craft as best you can, the value will come naturally. You will be in the space of doing what feels natural to you, comes natural to you, brings you immense joy and must therefore bring you immense value, naturally. As your value increases what you will receive increases. And yes, you will receive money as a subset of this abundance. And yes, you will realize although it is wonderful to have financial obligations met, it certainly is not on its own, fulfilling. For living in and with your currency is priceless.

Use the Energetic Invocations for *What is my currency?* as an activation tool to expand and organize your energy and move you into healthy, inspiring spaces. Comfortably contemplate them in stillness and silence, allowing the words and vibration to resonate into your cells. The invocations are guidelines to help you on your own journey so feel empowered to personalize them however you see fit.

What Is My Currency Invocations:

1. *I am of value and can never be defined by another's definition of value, for me.*

2. *I honor my currency and definition of exchange, and thus, others honor it.*

3. *I recognize when my exchange is out of alignment and I respect myself enough to exit the transaction or I renegotiate based upon my original definition of currency.*

Volume 7: What is my level of commitment?
Passion

- Is it bad to be committed to something or even someone?

Committed could be defined as having passion, yet it could also mean to be dedicated, engaged or obligated. You must be committed to yourself and to the realization of your potential, at any and all costs. If you have been doing the work and following the progression of this book, you are ready to be here at this point. You are revisiting who you are and your journey, with introspection and gratitude. You are learning that the only thing to take personal is yourself.

You must have a level of commitment to yourself because you are here. You have already agreed to be here, otherwise you would not be here. Yes, it is that simple, and you have a choice:

- You can commit to your reality, or
- You can commit to someone else's reality.

Process this:

> *As a child, we arrive and see what we see. Once we are old enough to understand we are given the rules of living here. We are told what is and is not possible. We are given a role with the expectation to fulfill it. Now, we are awakening. We realize that what we see is what we have been shown, but it is not what really is. We choose to continue to be in that space and time, or we choose to challenge and relinquish those roles, and explore what our own reality can really be.*

Look at what you have committed to already, regardless of whether you want to face it or not. Are you committed to a child, a sibling, a parent, a caretaker, a career or a story? Do you find yourself committed to fixing everyone's problems? If so, do the people learn, change and grow or are you just allowing others to depend on you, so you can manage their needs and fears?

- If this is where you are existing, is it truly your passion?

Passion should not be derived from being needed. If you operate from need, you lose who you are and become disconnected. Your commitment collapses and the relationship that bears unreasonable responsibility becomes just as unhealthy as the dependent one that gets angry when you are not there to repair everything. Rising to the occasion and facing challenges and obstacles is a part of living your own journey. By comparing your pursuits to others' you are embracing lack and judgment. There is no need to explain yourself and your life. Acknowledge that and be aware and committed to yourself, rather than waiting for others to acknowledge you. Move out of your comfort zone to have more passion, no matter how difficult it is. If you do nothing, nothing happens. Can you afford not to embrace something new, something different?

Process this:

Sometimes readers at this point will question whether their "new" world can truly exist. Here's a glimpse into the future: you will constantly challenge the situations and experiences and whether you can exist in this other world. If you think about your passion and what really makes you feel alive and compare it to what you "thought" was real, there is no comparison. This new and truer vision will tell you it is possible, through your commitment and how that feels.

Your level of commitment:
- is related to where your passion is, and
- is what propels you into the life you desire and are working towards.

Your level of commitment diminishes when tied:
- to fitting into someone else's story, and
- to living your life in reaction to everyone else.

Process this:

> *In reviewing articles and interviews by activists much like Gloria Steinem, Martin Luther King Jr., and Mahatma Gandhi, we noticed that these people created life-altering changes because they followed their passion, despite the challenges thrown in their faces. Activists like these started off hearing everyone around them comment: "You can't do that, you can't change anything. That is the way it has always been." But they were compelled to follow their beliefs. They were so passionate that they not only convinced themselves of their reality, but could also convince others to believe as they did.*

Even Socrates, a Greek Philosopher, reminded us to: 'Know Thyself,' in order to understand more about who we are, our commitments and our passions. Realize now that anything is possible, when we commit to our expertise and succeed in every way we choose, regardless of the conditions or stories of anyone else.

For, when you are open to seeing who people are, you find that their stories are not who they truly are. Seeing them for who they are is your level of commitment to others. You see them, when they are at their lowest and at their best. Nevertheless, you see the person, and to acknowledge and be present with that, without judgment, is a gift. So attune yourself to seeing the person and not the story. In turn, people will come back to you because they know they are being seen. Because when you see them, you will create further awareness and change.

Process this:

> A teacher teaching English abroad was given Class B when he arrived. To him Class B meant simply that he had a group class. But managers and other teachers soon visited him to apologize that he would be teaching this class, because they noted that the "B" actually stood for "brain dead." They further explained that the students in Class B could not speak English or carry on a conversation. The teacher was appalled at their description and was excited about teaching the students and having them share more about their culture. He decided to find a unique selling point in each student and manage the class by challenging them. After a few weeks, the students of Class B were laughing and joking in English, much to the surprise of the managers and teachers. By seeing, acknowledging and being present with them, the teacher was able to move the students beyond their own limited beliefs and everyone else's.

Your commitment to yourself is to see yourself for who you are and are working hard to become. It is about you showing up for yourself with passion and perseverance by taking a position, sticking to it by being consistent and by not dividing yourself between how much you want to invest in your existence and in this world, for any reason.

A synopsis of the tale of Hakuin, an old Japanese Zen Master, further explains commitment to oneself. Neighbors praised Hakuin for living a pure life, consistent with commitment. When a beautiful Japanese girl was found with child, Hakuin was incorrectly named the father, and his only comment was: "Is that so?" With a shattered reputation, Hakuin took care of the child for a year. Later the Japanese girl named a young fish market clerk as the father. Her parents apologized to Hakuin, and asked for forgiveness when they went to get their grandchild back. Hakuin's only reply was: "Is that so?"

Much like 'so what?' or 'what of it?', 'is that so?' garnished the passion of Hakuin's commitment to who he was, regardless of the circumstance or what others accused and judged of him. With these three words, Zen Master Hakuin remained committed to the true presence of himself, passionately integrated that into his environment, and operated from that space. Finally, the truth was revealed and others saw Hakuin's true self as well. So, see yourself and act from that valuable space, and others will see you.

Keep commitment active in your life by:
- being responsible for your actions in every minute,
- deciding to make it a priority every day, and
- exhibiting it as an example and model for others, without expectation.

The core of you is who you are. Being committed to you, in every waking, breathing moment is presence. It is presence for You. No longer continue to evaluate everything and then get stuck in analysis. Instead, utilize each discretion as an opportunity to deepen your commitment. Because this journey is just for you and was designed and created especially for you, only you. Be committed and be passionate, don't run away and don't hide. Be present and bask in your own existence while being committed to a life filled with presence for yourself and others.

Use the Energetic Invocations for *What is my level of commitment?* as an activation tool to expand and organize your energy and move you into healthy, inspiring spaces. Comfortably contemplate them in stillness and silence, allowing the words and vibration to resonate into your cells. The invocations are guidelines to help you on your own journey so feel empowered to personalize them however you see fit.

What Is My Level Of Commitment Invocations:

1. I am committed to the realization of my potential.

2. *Healthy, positive, purposeful commitment is to myself, based on truths, not lack, misconceptions or misplaced influences.*

3. *Keeping my focus on the goal, I do not get distracted by any untruths.*

4. *I retain and exhibit my commitment to its fullest, with unwavering commitment to myself, my life and my world at all times, without exception.*

Volume 8: What can my experience do for me?
Possibility

- All experience is learning, which opens you up to possibility.
- Possibility is everywhere.

For an experience to occur some kind of orderly change must happen. An environment with chaotic energy has continuous movement that is random and not often distinct experience. An environment with ordered energy has no change and no experience because there is no movement. Somewhere between the two, experience occurs when extreme chaos and order interact and the resulting energy opens up new waves of possibility.

Process this:

In total chaos all is random and meaningless. In total order everything is sterile and stagnant. So therefore, embrace your life with its ups and downs and its quiet times, as it moves between chaos and order.

As science has recognized thoughts as waves of energy, the sensations, feelings and emotions that you process are parts of experience. Being aware of waves basically helps you perceive experience and generating or stopping waves changes experience. With your thoughts affecting your experience, you may change your life, by changing your thoughts.

Process this:

Every morning, a woman found her husband moody and in despair about how he felt his life had been focused into a menial 9 to 5 job. She knew her husband was a conscientious, hard-worker who just hated the daily grind and commute, because once he was at work, he was happy to be in a social and productive environment. Yet she dreaded mornings because no matter how jovial she acted there seemed to be no change in the moody routine. Awakening one morning, she decided to picture her husband happy and excited. To her surprise and delight, he was. There was no other change in their daily routine except for her thoughts, which truly did affect her experience.

Did you ever wonder how certain people fill their lives with power and influence? Did you ever wonder why some people seem to be 'lucky?' Look closer and you will find that what and how you think experiences are, is nothing but an illusion. Some people are masters at creating elaborate illusions for their reality while others are but only players in those masters' creations.

Process this:

Daily our minds create perception as our brains interpret raw information. Science notes that only a few key elements are encoded in our memories and when retrieved, memories change, are reconstructed and re-stored, changed. So, what we see, experience and remember is a mere fragment of what actually occurs. Illusions, whether created by mentalists, magicians, or people around us, use the power of our minds and memory against us.

Understanding what an illusion is and what it isn't is helpful when understanding experiences. If you believe an illusion to only be a misinterpretation of your senses then you are missing the real magic.

An illusion is:
- an elaborate blend of stories and characters,
- a scenario created from beliefs, yours or another's, and
- connected to its creator.

Process this:

> *Illusions are created by the media, which influences others to see what they want you to see. The cup is half full or half empty. Both are true, but how you define and shape that truth heavily influences how you interpret other ideas and aspects around you. Have you ever walked into a new job, excited for something different, and the person training you tells you there is never enough time to do the work and that the bosses never appreciate anyone? And before you even have your first interaction, you are already defensive, or at a minimum, waiting for someone to say something that alludes to the truth of what you were told. Have you ever met someone with a reputation of being a phenomenal worker, very smart and very well connected? One businessman forced his illusions through words and stories. His elaborate tales were often repeated and shared at business meetings and with colleagues. Based on nothing but his words, colleagues started believing his qualifications, escapades and successes, often sharing them with others. In turn, he was extolled as an exemplary businessman, even though the proof was solely his own words which others allowed to create their reality. The employees tried to impress the businessman when all the while the businessman was using their work to impress and maintain his illusion with others. He was a grand master of illusion.*

Being interconnected, people observe and affect the world of reality. Creating it with an intention colored by experience and an emotion addicted to drama, we observe our lives in myriads of illusions. We may find our lives overflowing with abundant happiness or distraught with mayhem. We predict the outcome and then create that reality.

Much like our own reality, clouds of probability exist in limbo, until we observe them and make assumptions and predictions about them. In certain interpretations of quantum theory, quantum systems exist as the same clouds of probability until an observer predicts the outcome. Erwin Schrodinger, an Austrian Physicist and contemporary of Albert Einstein, presented a hypothetical experiment where a cat sat inside a box with a poison capsule, which may or may not be randomly ingested, thus determining whether the cat lived or died. Schrodinger hoped this hypothetical experiment would exemplify how ridiculous quantum theory was, because it predicted that an outcome was only reached once it was observed. In fact, the reality is that the cat is in a state of limbo, both alive and dead, because no one was observing its interaction with the poison capsule. Only with observation is the cat either dead, or alive. With observation, we too create the experience, outcome and illusion.

Process this:

In the example above, the cat could be alive or the cat could be dead. Adding the element of the observer creates the reality. If you observe the cat dead, it is dead. If you observe the cat alive, it is alive. If you are not there, there is no observer, it is in limbo, and no outcome is created. Don't get caught on the cat being dead or alive, the focus should be on the "in limbo," because then anything is possible. A college student interviewed for two jobs and did really well during the interviews. Knowing she would hear soon, she hoped she wouldn't get one so the decision would be easier. But why would she limit her possibility? The decision was in limbo and all she had to do was take the information and experience and hold onto it for the time being, knowing that in two weeks she would receive two job offers. At that point, she would have all the information she would need, and maybe information she would never dream she would have, and thus, would be able to make the best decision for her. So reviewing and mulling over the decision without all the information was creating a reality that didn't exist. When the decision was ready to be made, she would be a part of creating the outcome.

Whether out of maliciousness or not, people who create illusions will find a place for you within them. So, understand how illusions are presented to you. You decide whether or not you play a role or participate in them, but don't become lost in someone else's illusion.

Your degree of participation depends only upon your belief system, and the level at which you choose to participate. So, do you want to play in someone else's illusion or create your own reality?

Know that either choice or even fluctuating between both, depending upon the circumstances, is okay. As long as you have clarity, then you decide with awareness. Like a child, you may choose to play in someone else's game. Laugh, joke and watch experiences unravel, but once a game turns tragic or out of control, get out of it, or if it appears this way at the onset choose not to play. By being aware that situations and experiences are an illusion, you will choose to either ascend or fall deeper within the illusion.

Ironically, in the movie *"Forrest Gump,"* Tom Hanks portrayed a man that lived simply, yet still found himself a participant in the most intense illusions. As a story, it emphasized how one character can work with what is placed before him, without ever truly committing to the illusion. Forest Gump chose to do what he wanted, when he wanted. He did what his passion was, and when he was finished, he moved on to something different. People chased him, teased him, and were confused by him yet were also inspired by him. He chose to do what he wanted and nothing more or less while he moved from one experience to the next all the while being open to possibility.

Like Forrest Gump, there is nothing wrong with playing in illusions to help you do something for yourself. The Universe is abundant so there is plenty for everyone to entertain their goals and desires. If you are passionate, committed, strong and serious about your beliefs, and the kind of life you want to live, you will find many people playing roles in your illusions. And like children, the more people that play with you, the more fun it becomes and the more the illusion becomes real.

By using or creating an illusion, you are making a decision to enact a belief structure and project that into your environment to create a space of experience and possibility that will be aligned with your presence. Creating one which benefits you ensures that it is not to the detriment of anyone else. For example, when creating a business, if you plan to do your best for yourself and your customers, they will be satisfied and return, and your business will be a success. But if you go into business to put someone out of business, or to capitalize on someone else's hard work, you will never truly succeed. You may get money, but your level of commitment to yourself will be denigrated, your true passion interrupted and your possibilities will negatively affect your experiences.

Process this:

> The companies that survive and thrive are the ones that were built to improve life for all of us. These companies put some of our greatest artists, inventors and teachers into action. These are the businesses, thoughts and ideas that have been built upon over the years. The second tier companies, ones constructed to cash in on someone else's hard work, or set up to destroy competition, do not last the test of time. Even companies that were set up to create something new and improved for mankind, which over time lost their focus and mission, fall. Make your dream, goal and mission in alignment with your best interests and follow through. If you focus on your idea and creation, you will benefit and so will others whose lives will be improved by your accomplishments.

If you do not entertain pure possibility to elevate your experience, you will be stuck, asking:
• Why isn't this working?
• What am I not doing or doing incorrectly?

Take the leap and freefall into possibility to find what your experiences can do for you. For even the bumblebee confidently soars into flight, not minding that the laws of aerodynamics prove that it should not be able to fly. Yet the possibility exists, so not knowing it should not be able to fly, the bumblebee flies anyway. Using your own thoughts, intents and energies for momentum, you too can move beyond what you are told and often blindly follow. It is about time you pushed the probabilities to possibilities to create wondrous illusions of realities that empower you and those around you.

> •*If you only see what you or others believe is possible, you are not in possibility.*

Process This:

> Remember people are uncomfortable when you shake up their world with new beliefs. When you set your sights beyond what others have done or have believed is possible, you begin to think differently. Possibility means anything can happen. Don't define the end or outcome based solely on what you think you know. There are so many other things at play. Don't believe illusions because they pull you away from possibility. Sometimes what you don't know is more powerful, more potent. So just be open to that.

Reflect and then perceive, because finding your passion and creating your experience is a very personal journey. Do not condense its importance to only making money. For when you find your expertise and commit to it, you will notice yourself in magnificent places without realizing how you got there. People will begin to see you in ways that you might not have ever imagined. True none of that is actually personal, but you do have the power to create an illusion that is fun to play in and will allow different experiences to change you.

Use the Energetic Invocations for *What can my experience do for me?* as an activation tool to expand and organize your energy and move you into healthy, inspiring spaces. Comfortably contemplate them in stillness and silence, allowing the words and vibration to resonate into your cells. The invocations are guidelines to help you on your own journey so feel empowered to personalize them however you see fit.

What Can My Experience Do For Me Invocations:

1. I always live in possibility.

2. I will not limit myself to what I've been told.

3. Nothing is set in stone, anything can change, at any given moment. People, places and things may be predictable, however the Universe is never predictable.

Once you know and understand these concepts, step up and don't perpetuate what is not in your benefit or to the benefit of others. Know how powerful your spoken words are and how powerful your journey is. And now, you are a responsible adult for what you say to people in your environment, what you bring to the table with your journey and what you create to experience. It is time to stop unhealthy cycles, be responsible and learn, grow and change.

Part Three – People

Volume 9: How do I perceive relationships?
Intent

From experiences and how you live and perceive your life, you generate relationships. Relationships are always with you and help you excel when they operate from harmony in thought and action and nurture opportunities for you to know yourself more. Relationships help you learn lessons that open up interpretation and understanding. The lessons are not about what you are doing but rather about how you grow.

Every relationship you engage in helps you grow, expand, and learn, if that is what you choose. You exist as who you are in relationship to everyone and everything around you. Your relationships could be with friends, family, partners, coworkers, cashiers, bank clerks, teachers, landlords or even strangers. Every relationship is defined by people coming together with intent. There could be goals, exchanges, purposes, or just small interactions.

Nevertheless, with relationships, no matter the kind or reason:
- The one who stands before you, in every relationship, is a mirror of yourself.
- Your reflection is projected to you for you to learn from the interaction.

Process this:

An elderly woman spent a huge part of her time saying this person or that person irked and bothered her. She didn't like the woman two houses down from her because she was a gossiper, she didn't like the man across the street who offered to do things for her because she thought he was a shyster. The elderly woman never had anything nice to say about anyone when she, herself, was the gossiper and only asked for everyone to treat her like family so she could get special deals and discounts. She was not a happy person and never realized that what she was seeing and experiencing was a reflection of herself. Instead of

> looking at herself to fix her unhappiness, every person she met consistently reflected her own miserable self. You say what you need to hear. What you are experiencing is what you get out of it, and yes, this is a personal situation. Not what someone says to you but what you are supposed to learn from what you hear. When someone says something that irks or bothers you, your first response should be what do I need to hear from this. It wouldn't bother you if it wasn't something you didn't like about yourself, or what you needed to address.

Our interactions teach us to understand each other and ourselves, and since we are all connected, we can ask ourselves:
- *What do I want when I engage in a relationship?*
- *What is important when I am participating in a relationship?*
- *What is really required for me to have a relationship?*

Relationships may be laced with stories, judgments, heartaches, inspirations and a whole lot of 'he said' and 'she said' confrontations. Yet, being connected, we all share the energy of the relationships in which we choose to engage. Experiences open possibility and when we move outside of spaces we know, we then see, hear, and participate differently. Reactions are based upon how the relationship affects us. We may fall into a combination of dramas in our head before even meeting or we may choose to stay present, open and free to whatever occurs. For the dynamics may dissect, impinge, destroy or enable but always enlighten all parties.

Process this:

> We grow from chaos and interactions, how else do we create, manage and grow?

All this is important, simply for the perceptions you will have. Otherwise, if you lived in a box and had no interactions, you would not have relationships, and thus not move, change, or grow. You would stay the same without anyone to challenge your thoughts, ideas, actions, or existence. And as we all affect each other, we change individually and then again as a group.

For, when you add people to your life:
- you add their experiences, struggles, victories, heartbreaks and loves;
- you change the noise factor of your own environment;
- it becomes more eclectic as experiences become meaningful and enriching; and
- you allow more relationships to question your own perception.

Process this:

We are here for each other to help each other learn and grow. On our own, our experiences are limited. Interactions enrich our own lives, for better or for worse. As much as people drive each other crazy, if you take people out of the mix the color of our lives would be lost.

Anthropologists, sociologists and psychologists agree that we are social beings and that relationships spice up our lives. Yet, predictable beings are boring and no relationship is ideal. If we find ourselves wondering if someone likes us or has fun when we are around, perhaps we are being too predictable. We must remember that each interaction reveals more about ourselves yet it is not personal.

Interactions benefit you, especially when a friend cannonballs you into a new place, with a new outlook and outlandish experiences. Sluggish energy can help you move forward, too, if you understand it and see it for what it is. But when others fail to add value to the exchange because they only attach to your energy, or want you to do the work, and you oblige, neither party benefits.

If it feels like you are accumulating someone else's judgments, concerns and gripes, remember:
- you should not be attaching yourself or allowing others to attach to you,
- what your relationships say, think and do does not matter, and
- what you *perceive* your relationships say, think and do does matter, because that is what you believe, ingest and incorporate into your life.

Process this:

A receptionist for a small company greets each person with a: "Good morning! How can I help you?" Ten people receive this greeting and each one experiences it differently. One may be inspired by its warmth, another decides it is phony and is bothered by it, and another feels it is needy and intrusive. So each of these ten people incorporates the energy of what they perceived into their experience, and moves forward with that energy into the rest of their day. The actual words, experiences and events in a relationship don't matter. What you take away from all of those is what matters. So be weary of what you take away, because that is what is important.

In healthy relationships everyone moves with the energy and responsibly does the work because the force comes from agreements, disagreements and hearty exchanges, rather than sitting still. Relationships challenge you to constantly evaluate and analyze whether your best interests are being served. When you meet this head on, you are exhibiting self-care for yourself and are not being narcissistic or self-obsessed. Realize that it is important for you to constantly feel comfortable yet open to uncertainty, to stay in the presence of you, being fully alive.

So, ask:
- *How does this relationship enhance my own learning?*
- *When I partake in this exchange am I exhibiting self-care?*

Often, relationships become too structured, filled with to do's that match other people's definition of what a relationship is. As with everything, relationships become measured by others' illusions. Feeling the pressure to be like those searching for or showing you what a 'real' relationship is, you struggle with the obligation to be like everyone else. However, moving out of obligation and back into intent gives you power. So, what is your intent and what do you really want?

<u>Process this:</u>

> *You can choose the who, how and when of a relationship at any time. Most people say this is done through boundaries and we agree. However, boundaries do not need to be spoken, enforced, or rigid. You create your boundaries energetically and in your own mind. It is not an external practice, it is an internal practice. The boundary is not in what someone is allowed to say and do. The boundary is how far they can influence your thoughts moods and direction.*

Participate in a relationship or don't. Whatever your decision, do what you want, the way you want. Stop funding someone else's illusion. Genuinely invest your time in others and connect, acknowledge and embrace their importance as well as your own. Take back your power and move to clear intent.

Ask yourself, over and over again:
- *What is my perception of this relationship and what is my intention?*

There are many coexisting relationships in nature. So look to nature for instruction. Some elements help each other while others ignore each other, choosing what is best for their situation. But all work together, directly or indirectly. By investigating the myriad of relationships in nature and science, we can further comprehend our own. Scientifically there are four symbiotic relationships:

- when both species benefit from the interaction, and there is an exchange and flow (called mutualism),
- when two different species associate and one benefits while the other is harmed (called parasitism),
- when two different species associate and one enjoys a benefit while the other is not significantly affected (called commensalism), and
- when two organisms of different species associate and one is inhibited or killed, during competition for resources, while the other is unaffected (called amensalism).

As the species described above are energy, we are too, and have similar interactions. Regardless of the names of the symbiotic interactions, each one may be compared with how we all interact, resulting in beneficial or detrimental outcomes with each other. Thus, if we are focused with clear intent to grow and learn, a mutualistic exchange would create the most benefit. For a tree does not get upset, as a person would, when another tree appears next to it. Yet, we often speak of having our space, setting boundaries, and creating exclusive groups which restrict others, to keep energies away. As we are all energy and connected, there really are no barriers needed to protect ourselves, except those of which we do not let go.

Process this:

In an office, a secretary has been loudly planning her wedding, creating a level of frustration and chaos for her coworkers. Each one deals with the situation differently: the manager simply instructs the secretary to focus on her work and stop the chatter; the marketing assistant laughs and attends to her business; the bookkeeper, however, tries to ignore it, envisions a pink bubble of calm and protection around herself and thinks productive thoughts, even though she remains bothered. Unbeknownst to the bookkeeper, she has just set it center stage in her life by allowing it to affect her. The bookkeeper has created a barrier, and ironically taken it in, allowing it to affect her mood and direction. As we are all energy, we are all connected. And being connected, barriers therefore cannot exist. If there is something that is said or occurs which upsets you, by allowing it to pass by, and not holding onto it, does it not affect you, similar to the actions of the manager and marketing assistant. It is when you stop it (and create a barrier) that it affects you emotionally or physically, similar to the bookkeeper. It's as if you created a parking space for it, next to your seat. So, not only are you not required to put up barriers, but should you put one up, you should also ask, why did you place the barrier, and is there an issue you are holding onto yourself?

As a wave separates from the ocean and journeys to the shore, it meets other waves, intersecting and blending, while moving beyond, rather than strong arming other waves as foes. Instead, each wave returns to the ocean whole and fresh, taking the exchange, letting it go, and moving ahead with how it has changed. There is no need, no competition, nor lack of space or energy, for energy is unlimited, with both nature and us.

- Demanding to have a need fulfilled is not experiencing a relationship or the healthy aspects of energy.
- Neediness is just an excuse for an easy way out and an expectation that someone else will do the work for you.
- If you are making the demands, reevaluate your intent and step up for yourself.
- If someone else is making the demands stop enabling them.
- When a relationship feels out of synchronization, it is up to you to move beyond beliefs, expectation and guilt, and go to the truth of the situation.
- Take responsibility for yourself and be honest, aware and committed, rather than blaming yourself or others.

- Only by asking for the truth can you evaluate the multitude of options you have.

In finding the truth, you must first understand that you or another has created this illusion and has placed you and others inside of it, much like a child playing in a sandbox. If a child invites you to play in her sandbox, you can choose to play and have fun with her toys and enjoy the illusion; or decide not to play, if you don't feel like it. For a child, it's a simple choice, to play in the sandbox or not, play together or not, based upon what both want to do. It is not personal. Both can say goodbye and look for someone else to play with who wants to do the same.

As adults, do we do this? Not as long as our intent is laced with reasons other than what we want to do. We make assumptions about judgments, like being excluded or excluding others. We want to get even, we want revenge, we want to help, etc. We don't base our decision on simply what we would like to do. This is perhaps where everything goes awry.

Process this:

A group of friends go to an amusement park, and once through the entry gate, they grab maps. A few decide to wait in line at the roller coaster, others decide to grab fried dough and French fries, two decide to play in the arcade, and one doesn't even take the map, telling the others she doesn't care, and that she will just go wherever everyone else wants to go. Which one are you? Are you doing what you want to do with reckless abandonment, or is it laced with other reasons? Don't not do something because you don't like who is doing it. Do what you want to do regardless of what anyone else says, does, thinks or feels and give others the freedom to do the same.

Also, be aware that if you are the one doing the inviting, the other person may have declined because she may have just played for hours in someone else's sandbox, may not enjoy sand or playing in sandboxes, or may prefer playing with dolls instead. There is no drama to assign, only that she is not interested in doing what you are doing. In seeking to learn more about yourself through relationships, you also enter a vulnerable place, but there too, you can find your power.

By determining whether the invitation to experience a relationship is purely from need or if it is with the intent of a healthy, mutual exchange is important for your self-care. Decide about your participation, and be confident, powerful and energized by your action. But don't maliciously attack the other person if you decide not to engage in their illusion. Choose to move on with love and gratitude, otherwise you make it personal and create 'story.' For, when both parties operate from clear intent, both freely and maturely accept or decline participation, without attachment.

We must realize in each and every interaction:
- There is nothing personal about it unless you make it personal.
- Most often others are caught up in assumptions and judgments, so that they do not even see you because they are talking to themselves, can only hear themselves, and are completely unaware of your presence.
- Most of our interactions are based in conversation. Ask who is speaking, who they are actually talking to and who is being heard.

Process this:

> A classic joke goes like this:
> Three elderly women are out walking. The first says: "It is windy today, isn't it?" The second one says: "No, it's Thursday." The third one says: "Thirsty? Me too! Let's go get a drink!"
> Who is talking and who is being heard?

Know that there are some people who only feel alive by stirring up havoc in others' lives. However, the only way they can do that is if we allow them the space to do it.

So, how do we disallow others the space to create this havoc?

1. Have clarity and be clear about what is happening. Focus on your awareness.

2. Understand they have no power, not just over you, but over the interaction. They are hoping you will give them power, because on their own they are powerless. Similar to an inflated balloon, the minute you stop adding air to the balloon, it deflates.

3. Choose you. Initially it appears their story trumped as you did not entertain any story, including your own. Since you did not entertain any story these people can no longer hook into you and create havoc for you. You are not interacting in their story so they, and their stories deflate. As they become unsure of what happened, they may look for a new source to tempt or may just sit dumbfounded. They have chosen not to do their own work. There is no longer an obligation on your part, not that there ever was. Your journey (and lessons gleaned) is complete with them. Let them go with love and kindness, understanding that something better is waiting for you up ahead.

4. Do not look back or allow guilt to bring you back. Focus on gratitude for what you have learned and for whatever else you received in the interaction.

Process this:

> High School Reunions tend to create anxiety, feelings of inferiority and concerns regarding falling back into old, dysfunctional roles, regardless of being the Prom Queen, Jock, Geek or Wallflower. How do we not fall back into these roles, not allowing these people to create havoc in our lives? The steps could be as follows:
> 1. It is a High School Reunion! Go or don't go – if it is not enjoyable, don't go; if it could be fun, then go. It's fun to see and be seen, without obligation or expectation.
> 2. There may be those there who hope they can appear more successful, better looking, or happier than you. They can only succeed in this if you participate in their game. You know who you are, you know we all come from the same source, and you know nobody is better or worse, we just express ourselves differently. The game is boring, and you can just smile when the situation arises rather than entertain feelings of story.
> 3. By simply smiling when others boast, you may initially feel like they made their point and they now think they are better than you. You did not entertain their story, create one of your own, or barricade yourself. You are completely free of their influence over you. None of the stories stuck with you.
> 4. Now you know, so you can look back upon High School for what it was: a learning experience for both positive and negative. However, you can never look back and entertain new thoughts of anxiety and feelings of inferiority, etc. anymore.

To let someone go with love and kindness, you must acknowledge what you received in the interaction, and have gratitude. You must also be clear that whatever happened, that ended the relationship, had to occur, to be sure that both parties knew the interaction was complete. Denying what happened and creating excuses only prolongs the process and the pain. Further growth is put on hold. In understanding the differences in expectations, without making it personal, the real truth can be found. The person will disconnect, with kindness and can freely go. If you are the one unable to let go of someone with love and kindness, you need to dive deeper into reflection, without personalizing it, until you feel this understanding, and a disconnection, without anger, hurt or resentment. This is an important exercise and eventually you will succeed in understanding. You will find that most of the people you let go with love will go on their way, or will start to see and value you differently. At this point, it is your choice to embrace the new relationship or not. Beware though, if you start to devalue yourself or fall into old habits, the relationship will become dysfunctional, again.

If you begin to perceive all your relationships this way, you start to envision the structure of relating that exists around and through you. Take the opportunity now to get that.

- Once you change how you view relationships, you can actually create them instead of being reactive to the same situations.
- Remember that others perceive you as a part of their relationship and quite often to them, you are not who you are, but who they perceive.
- Be prepared for all kinds of interactions, some even unfamiliar, knowing they are always in your best interest.
- Be aware of what you are perpetuating and encourage your best interests.
- Take comfort in just being in the moment.

Show up for yourself and choose to have a whole, healthy relationship. Stay in the present moment and naturally go to the truth of every interaction.

Use the Energetic Invocations for *How do I perceive relationships?* as an activation tool to expand and organize your energy and move you into healthy, inspiring spaces. Comfortably contemplate them in stillness and silence, allowing the words and vibration to resonate into your cells. The invocations are guidelines to help you on your own journey so feel empowered to personalize them however you see fit.

How Do I Perceive Relationships Invocations:

1. I am surrounded by people like me. I let go of judgment and personal stories.

2. I allow others to be who they choose to be and value each one to the extent they impact my life.

3. I am clear in all transactions and understand that nothing is personal nor is anything to be taken personally.

4. I define my relationships.

5. There is no limitation on the possibilities always available to me in each and every interaction.

6. Although a situation may appear to be fixed or out of control, the Universe and its infinite options are never predictable.

7. I am responsible for the energy behind each communication in which I engage.

8. I allow each new relationship to stand on its own merits without a preconceived past, present or future.

9. I realize that an existing relationship is recreated at every opportunity.

10. The Universe makes all things even by placing all people and events exactly where they should be.

Volume 10: Will love make me whole?

Wholeness

Love is being in a shared, sacred space where both participants are comfortable and safe.

Process this:

> *How has love been defined? It has been defined through movies, love songs written about unrequited love, and sonnets passed down through the years. We all end up thinking love has to come out of drama, turmoil, or even a need to be rescued. It has even been turned into a business, as we choose to celebrate Valentine's Day, or not, much like a birthday or holiday. What if love transcended all of that and was simply being in a relationship with another who put you at ease because you both mutually cared for each other and enjoyed each other's company. You can just love somebody, and that is it.*

When you realize the power of this shared, sacred space, and how it can affect you, ask yourself:

- *Is this kind of love in my life right now?*
- *Does the love around me, right now, take me into that sacred space?*
- *When I say "I love you," do I always mean it from that space?*
- *When I experience love and loving someone, am I in that shared space?*

"Love is of all passions the strongest, for it attacks simultaneously the head, the heart and the senses," according to Lao Tzu, in the *"Tao Te Ching."* As our head encompasses our intellect, it works along with the heart to direct our senses. So when our hearts are touched, we begin to discover the limitless warmth and gentleness of our being. Our head erupts in signals that pulsate our cells, interact with our senses, open our hearts more and connect us with others.

In continuing to open our hearts with loving kindness, we have the choice to love ourselves. By moving past bitterness, anger, resentment, fear and despair, we can pour compassion into our expanded consciousness and open up to receiving love and loving others and ourselves. In that pure moment, we know love and make our existence more intense. As two wholes come together in a relationship based upon mutual trust, respect, integrity, understanding, and truth, something greater is created and there is no need. If need appears, lack appears and the love is diminished by guilt, expectation and obligation.

Love is:
- an opportunity to see and learn about yourself, with another,
- based in energy, vibration, and light, which manifests itself in the physical,
- like the wind, because it exists via interpretation and sensations, and
- a sacred space to be in and shared with whomever or whatever is important to you.

Love is not:
- feelings of obligation when the focus is on need and chaos,
- making someone happy or someone making you happy,
- an all-encompassing obsession to fill a void, and
- a commodity to barter, sell or exchange, when another's sacred space is at stake.

Process this:

Are you a prince searching for a princess? Are you hoping someone can make you feel good about yourself? Are you looking to get revenge on a past relationship? What if you have all you need? You don't need saving or fixing. The love you want doesn't come from deserving and can come without all that drama.

Everyone experiences love as it is not exclusionary or discriminating. Valuing its true presence is the same as recognizing the difference between a fast food restaurant and elegant dining. At a fast food restaurant, the meal may be quick, pre-processed, mostly unhealthy, questionably handled, and presented to you in the same manner you ordered, while zooming around the drive-thru. With elegant dining, your attire, the ambiance, the presentation, the actual food and the length of your meal affect your enjoyment. Either restaurant has food that can satisfy your hunger, but the value of its true presence and how it affects you, is different.

Similarly, everyone receives love, but may find they don't recognize its presence so they do not truly value it from where it is coming. If love does not come as or from whom you expected, it does not mean that love is not available. If you review your childhood, your school years, your adult life, or your current situation, can you recognize love in your life?

Love could come from:
- an animal or treasured pet that was always beside you,
- a child who loved to play games with you,
- a school friend or teacher who helped you,
- an Aunt, Uncle or distant cousin who favored you,
- a Grandparent who helped take care of you,
- an early girlfriend or boyfriend,
- a colleague or co-worker who mentored you,
- a partner who is always by your side,
- a good friend who always has your best interests at heart, or
- an older neighbor who shared wisdom with you.

Process this:

> Many times we take this love for granted. Since we don't appreciate it, we never see it.
> Where is the love you are taking for granted and therefore not seeing?

Recognizing and being open to love appearing in your life in different ways is important. For if you have been thinking that it is missing or will never be available for you, it has actually been there all along. It may have appeared in many different ways, shapes and forms, but it was there. None of us are new to experiencing it, only our perspectives are new.

Process this:

> A friend found herself connecting single friends and making successful matches. Yet, she remained single, desiring someone to fill the void she was feeling. She kept asking: "Why can't I find love?" All the while, love was all around her. She, herself, never saw that.

If the people around you, growing up, were not able to express love in the way you expected, you must understand, it had nothing to do with you. It was not a measure of your value or self-worth, because it was not personal. If you made it personal that was your interpretation, but it was not the truth. All the while, it was the other person who was incapable of expressing love, who was actually lacking self-love.

Open yourself up to the possibility of love:
- Be aware of love and allow it to be present in your life.
- Resonate with the feeling of love and integrate it.
- Don't be afraid to share the experience of love and who you are.

Process this:

> *Sometimes we meet someone who strikes a chord. That person makes us smile or laugh or just think. And the feeling we have is extraordinary. There is a bit of love in that feeling as it connects with the energy we experience. That space is also a doorway to possibility because the energy carries forward in your gait, your personality and throughout the rest of your day. The energy of love is all around us. Can you be adventurous enough to uncover even its simplest tones and allow it to bring you somewhere you may never have ventured? By interacting with that person who made you smile, laugh or just think, in a different and fun way, your presence changed.*

Choose to bring the possibility of this experience, with a partner, into your life. Clear space for the kind of love you desire. Remove any obligation or expectation and enjoy spontaneity and fun creating your space together. Realize the physical manifestation of love is a part of your relationship but not all of it. Love is sharing who you are without judgment or hesitation, and being comfortable in that space with each other. Love is understanding and accepting, and aligned with self-care.

Always be respectful of love showing up in your life, and exhibit self-care whether or not you decide to participate in the relationship. If you find yourself or someone else you have been involved with falling out of love, be respectful of that as well. Embrace that this is or was a relationship and that it was a part of your experience. See that, honor that, and when the time for it to end comes, let it go peacefully. Do not yearn for something (which focuses on lack) and do not have regrets (which focuses on continuation or unending). If the focus stays on lack or unfinished business, you cannot move into the next stage in your journey. If the relationship is over, be mature and responsible and let it go without malice or deceit. By eliminating what is not working for you, you make room in your life for future possibilities.

Ending a love relationship is no different than ending any relationship. It can, at times, be difficult as either you cannot move on, or the other person will not move on. So should this be the case, review your perception of relationships and the steps to moving past those trying to create havoc in your space.

Process this:

Ending any relationship is difficult and brings many feelings and emotions to the surface. Relationships come in and out of our lives, some for only mere moments, some months, years, or a lifetime, and there might be ones that we do not feel ready to let go of, but must. By honoring a relationship, you honor its ending, and accept that it was what it was meant to be. You must move forward, knowing that this now leaves an opening for something new.

By doing this, you will help yourself be aware of any and all blockages you may have to love.

Blockages to love may include:
- feeling unworthy and insecure,
- convincing yourself that there is no one out there for you,
- fearing love and what it might do to you as an independent person,
- insatiably needing love in lieu of receiving it, or
- carrying failed, past relationships around.

Process this:

A love interaction is no different than any other interaction we have with people. Our definition of love is not meant to be exclusively attributed to a romantic love. It can be applied to love between friends, parents and a child, siblings, aunts/uncles etc. You are limiting yourself if you only think of love in terms of having a significant other.

Granted, most of us have carried around many of these blockages when in pursuit of love. We have assigned them whatever meaning they have for us, even though the possibility of love always exists. So instead, why not:

- Focus on opening the shared, sacred space of love for you.
- Recall that love may not come as you expect or hope, but it is still ever-present.
- Love yourself in order to love someone else and to accept love.
- Open to love without condition or attachment.
- Remember that love is not about filling a need but is about mutual sharing.

Remember, the only way to conquer blockages is to go to the truth. Love is a huge part of our lives but we consistently operate from not having it. We then wonder if love will make us whole. No relationship will make us whole, except for the relationship we have with ourselves.

Use the Energetic Invocations for *Will love make me whole?* as an activation tool to expand and organize your energy and move you into healthy, inspiring spaces. Comfortably contemplate them in stillness and silence, allowing the words and vibration to resonate into your cells. The invocations are guidelines to help you on your own journey so feel empowered to personalize them however you see fit.

<u>*Will Love Make Me Whole Invocations:*</u>

1. I am perfect and whole and need nothing to complete me.

2. I let go of any preconceived ideas of what love should look like.

3. *Love is engaging at a level that is in alignment with self-care.*

4. *I embrace all the love around me.*

5. *I welcome a partner to enhance my experience, expansion and understanding of this world and my life.*

6. *The Universe is helping me to release old hurts and beliefs to fully embrace a true and healthy love in my life.*

7. *An empowering, enriching, healthy environment is supportive of my relationships and will continue to enhance them.*

Volume 11: Who are the people like me?
Predictability

Look in the mirror.
- Who are you?

Look around you.
- Who are the people around you?
- Are they like you?

The people like you might or might not be around you right now. If you feel supported and empowered you could be surrounded by the people like you. If you feel tired, listless and like you just don't fit in, you might not be around the people like you. But it is not just about what you are feeling. It is about who you are being, and if you are respecting who you are with your intent, words and actions.

If you have been doing the work consistently with this book then you have been learning who you are and are moving and expanding with clearer intent. Probably, you have also been recognizing the changes within and around you.

Process this:

You and other people change all the time. Therefore, nothing can be taken for granted and nothing is set in stone. If you are looking for the people like you, rule number one is that you can't say they are or are not around you. Maybe they were yesterday or they weren't. Today is a new day.

So, who are the people like you? Only you can answer that question. The people like you are there for you to help you learn your lessons. Somehow they are handpicked by you, chosen to show up at the right time and place to be there just for you. They push you to be your best, provide comfort, and support you in ways you may never have understood before.

The people like you do not present you with needs or obligations. They do not expect you to fill their deficits. If there is something missing in their life, whether it be energy, relationships or even direction, it is up to them to figure that out. It is not up to you to provide a comfortable space for them to practice and perform their life. All that running to the rescue and being available when it really doesn't work for you does not align with true self-care, while in the interim, your life disappears to the shadows. You then run the risk of missing the true intent of your life here, and fall into someone else's story.

Process this:

A Training Manager was deep into developing curriculum on her computer when she smelled Chinese food. Upon raising her head, she found the Marketing Director enjoying lunch in her office. Appalled, she asked him what he was doing. In the middle of a bite, he casually replied that her office was comfortable and the ambiance was much better than the breakroom. He further explained that his day had been stressful and he needed to feel better, and her office environment helped him to do that. Infuriated, she kicked him out. Unfortunately, the smell of his food lingered. It would not have been self-care for her to grin and bear his company just because her office offered him respite from the drama in his life. If she had allowed him to stay, it would have made her very uncomfortable and it would not have been in her best interests. It was not her responsibility to create that space for anyone, and it would not have helped him to create a dependency on her space.

People have used other people to create a wealth of drama surrounding events, to add to their stories. Good or bad, we often hear:
- "My family . . . me,"
- "I was victimized by . . .,"
- "He saved my life, so . . .,"

- "She was my hero . . .," and
- "What are you doing to me?"

When the above described events occur during your journey, there is always much to absorb and learn from them. Their significance extends far beyond drama, story, and personalization. So when the meaning becomes lost, these challenges just become story, to be rehashed over and over again. No storyline is a good storyline, unless it is for pure entertainment purposes, i.e. a Hallmark™ movie. In real life, when the story falls away the true substance and intent of the people involved are all that is left. When the divisions of people created by story fall away, we may finally realize that we are all no different from each other.

- So how do you get past story:

1. First realize that whatever the story is, it is just a story, and it has nothing to do with you.
   You could take that sadly, but there is no grief to be had. It simply has nothing to do with you, so stop taking it personally and stop making it personal.

2. Next, determine how you define your relationship and at what point you want to live in that person's story.
   What is your relationship to each other and does that person's story really work for you?

3. Then work for clarity to choose who you are in relation to their story.
   Are you a catalyst or an enabler?
   Do you start things and help them to keep moving, learning and growing, or do you just enable the other person to keep regurgitating their story?

4. Next, decide what you want to contribute to their story.
   Focus on understanding and awareness, not lack, guilt, vindication, or worry. In order to get past

vindication, take yourself out of the story. Remember that it has happened for you, not to you.

5. With new clarity, create your own story, one that works for you.
   Find yourself around others that inspire you and help you move to a new awareness. Embrace having the right people around you who support, encourage, and love you.

6. Remember, as storylines fall away, we may celebrate our similarities and differences with new understanding.
   Our journeys are wonderful opportunities to learn. Allow, receive and embrace unpredictability.

Process this:

A young bank teller was working just before a busy holiday weekend. The bank was full of people and everyone was mandated to take only a half hour lunch break, down from the normal hour long break. As this young teller closed her window to take her break, she walked in the back room to find the branch manager in tears. When she asked what happened, the branch manager explained the argument she had with another coworker, what had happened, how she felt and how she could not understand how it happened and how unfair the situation was for her. The teller spent her whole break listening to this manager tell her story, only at the end of the half hour to go back to her window and continue to service the huge amount of people in the lobby. There was no offer to take some more time to eat, or any remorse on the side of the branch manager. The teller did not practice self-care, and the branch manager ultimately stopped crying, but held tightly to her story.

A better way for the teller to get past the story and deal with the situation better could have been:
   1. Understand that the branch manager, although older and more experienced, was stuck in a story. The teller could have kept her perspective, listened but not added or detracted from what she was hearing. Feeling obligated to help as it was a work related issue created a responsibility that wasn't hers.

2. Once having the clarity of what was happening, the teller might have made a simple statement to extract her involvement with the story, and therefore closed the conversation.
3. She might have simply offered a statement that they could work it out, and not felt any guilt or sense of responsibility on her part. She was not a part of it and should not place herself in the story.
4. She takes her belongings and makes her way to the door, and enjoys her lunch break.
5. Now, as an adult, the teller understands better who she is and has more awareness.

Know that, if you choose you, and refuse to be a part of someone's story, you may be made to feel like you don't fit in. This is important as it is a form of bullying. This is adult bullying and it is what we, the adults, are modeling to the youth in society. Adults ridicule youth, criticizing them for being bullies and for lashing out against bullying, yet these same adults bully other adults, using various tactics to hold them to, in most cases, their own self-abusive stories. The pain behind bullying can be excruciating without a support system. When you understand that adult bullying is no different than the bullying on playgrounds, you must stay focused, and become comfortable knowing the real truth of the situation.

Process this:

Look at what is going on, in the media, in society and even in your own community, do you see bullying? If you don't, look again. Society judges and makes comments about childhood and teenage bullying and questions what is wrong with these young adults and what makes them become bullies. Never does anyone look at the adults who raise, teach, coach and set the example for these young adults. It is time for the adults to be adults and acknowledge our own bullying that happens at every level of society and work to change that. Only by addressing the real issue can we make a change. It is time to be the adults.

Regain your power by being you, show up and stand up for you. You will eventually come to a new space, and others' stories will seem boring and irrelevant. You will then start to create a story, for you, which embraces possibility. Others, ironically, will start to show up for you. The importance of finding the right people is only for you to answer, to the degree to which you choose. The right people are the real, genuine people who will enhance your true living. They are unpredictable and move with their intent to learn and grow, and just be, together.

In *"I Am,"* an American documentary by Tom Shadyac, it was revealed that our true nature is to work in cooperation with each other, proving that we ultimately want to be connecting with each other rather than competing with each other. Napoleon Hill, American author, further emphasized the importance of cooperation when he interviewed wealthy individuals in order to gather success strategies. Hill observed the Mastermind Principle, where an alliance of two, with more minds working together in perfect harmony, led to success in reaching a common goal. Through cooperation, the equation of $1+1=3$ becomes an exponential factor leading to connecting, networking and sharing best practices for prosperous results, where success is achieved in cooperative environments, as opposed to those with individuals competing against each other.

Even Neuroscience has illustrated the importance of cooperation, with the Hebbian Theory, which shows that cells that fire together, wire together. According to this theory, neurons in the brain perform together while learning occurs, and connections occur and remain, while those that are not required are eliminated. Likewise, people working conscientiously and cooperatively towards a common goal operate successfully together, while those lacking these cooperative environments become frustrated and tired. By finding the right people, we move into the most productive, cooperative environment to escalate our experiences and our journey with others.

Process this:

> We have all been on successful teams before and understand the benefits of working together. Science and history has shown that we perform at higher levels when we are connected and moving towards a common goal. It behooves us to do our best work and to really make an effort to reach out and find others who have that common goal.

So, how do you find the people like you?

1. Acknowledge the people that are not right for you in your life.
   You need to let them go with love, not regret, anger, or expectation of anything from them. The hardest part is in letting them go. That is a huge first step because in doing that you now open space.

2. Understand that the right people are around you all the time. You simply need to be open to them.
   Being open to new situations and relationships fosters new connections. As you practice self-care and abide by the definition of your currency exchange, you have set the standard for those who you will and will not invite into your space. This should be fun.

3. You cannot control the timing. You must trust that the right people are there.
   They will appear once you open to them. Sometimes it is just a matter of changing your focus and view. If your focus is always on the wrong people, the right people are in your peripheral vision. Bring the right people forward and push the wrong people to the background. It's all in how you see the picture!

As you are moving forward, never find yourself lost in a space of waiting. There is nothing and no one for which to wait. While you are elevating your awareness to the people like you and they are making their way to you, you should be working on yourself. Only then will you be a full, complete, self-actualized person ready to share a meaningful relationship, rather than one who is needy, waiting and expecting.

Find your true self. Go deeper and search out yourself in unchartered territory that is challenging and healthy. Ask questions using 'how?' rather than 'why?' In doing this, you open to pure magnificence, self-assured compassion and complete freedom. By having clear and inspired ideas about yourself and your life you can be comfortable exploring the grandest idea of who you could be, with humor and zest. So do not be afraid to be valiant and courageous when it comes to your own life, while also being filled with gratitude. You have value, you are important, you matter and your life is to be lived exclusively by you. Be open to what is unpredictable and be comfortable in the presence of uncertainty.

Use the Energetic Invocations for *Who are the people like me?* as an activation tool to expand and organize your energy and move you into healthy, inspiring spaces. Comfortably contemplate them in stillness and silence, allowing the words and vibration to resonate into your cells. The invocations are guidelines to help you on your own journey so feel empowered to personalize them however you see fit.

Who Are The People Like Me Invocations:

1. *As I truly know who I am, I create the definition of those I want around me.*

2. *Who I am affects who I am with. It is of utmost importance to be in alignment with intent.*

3. *I need to trust that my highest self knows better than my everyday self.*

4. *There are multitudes of people like me in my world.*

5. *Energizing and accentuating the true power of who I am, I draw abundance and opportunity, allowing me to pinpoint focus towards the people like me.*

6. *The way to find the people like me is to clearly put my intent out and be open minded to feeling the highest and best in my environment.*

7. *The people like me allow me to rise to the occasion and encourage me to be more of who I am, allowing me to grow and expand in a way that empowers me*

8. *The people like me do not hide behind me. They are clearly present, open and aware of my nature and they celebrate and compensate for it.*

9. *The people like me are always accessible around me and it is up to me to clearly see and acknowledge them at all times, being grateful.*

10. *The people like me accelerate and enhance my highest and best creativity, yet remind me of my connection with the All.*

Once you know how to survive with awareness in this world you can always find yourself amongst any group of people. Although you might not be able to control who is around you, you certainly can control with whom you share your space. Allow people of like vibration in your space but don't get caught in others' incompatible vibrations. If you don't want people in your vibration you simply don't invite them there. Those who are comfortable will resonate in your space and you may naturally open to them. Those who are not comfortable are not required to stay in your space. Be cordial if you so desire, and walk away. Then open up the space of your vibration and allow who you want in, those who align with who you are. As people thrive in comfortable vibrations, embrace the parts that are empowering and be involved. Always decide where you are comfortable and live from that space, that presence.

Part Four – Environment

Volume 12: How do I flourish in my environment?   *Space*

- Are you aware that you are creating your environment, right now?

Process this:

> One Mexican restaurant sits on the hill, and the other is closer to town. Both cater to a local crowd and serve traditional Mexican fare. So what could the difference be? The first has wait staff who reluctantly greet you at the door, haphazard tables with not enough chairs and a constant refrain: "We can't do that." They can't sit two people away from the door at a 4-chaired table because someone else may come. This may not be crucial, but it does affect the environment. For as they are not able to make decisions or make alternative plans, they stagnate themselves and their business. They do not have people anxious to eat there and the ones that are eating look oddly constipated and somewhat irate. The second Mexican restaurant has a hostess that is accommodating and friendly. She somehow addresses your concerns before they develop and finds a way to cheerfully greet every person who enters and quickly seat them, moving the flow of people constantly arriving to eat. Once you are at your table, an engaging waitress greets you, thanks you for being there, and continues to notice when your table needs any kind of attention. The environment bounces and flows with the energy that keeps so many customers coming back. Two Mexican restaurants, in the same town; two very different environments.

Energy is all around us, and we are a part of that energy, interconnected. Even science tells us that as energy connects everything in the universe it is also a part of what it connects. So as we interact energetically with each other, our space is a product of the energy we create and carry and the energy we allow to affect us. That energy includes everything and everyone we meet, think about, spend time with, experience and retain as part of our lives. And that energy travels everywhere, in thoughts, dreams, actions, speech and simple presence, creating the Universe. Remember, too, that our beliefs also affect ourselves, those who appear around us and, in turn, the space which we create as our environment.

Process this:

> When you say, "I can't do that," you stagnate the environment. Eventually, the environment will move around you, but no matter what you do, you can't escape yourself. So you better start thinking about things differently.

Science tells us that we are mainly space and that objects, themselves, have a vast distance of space between their particles. In *"What the Bleep Do We Know!?"*, a movie that investigates the quantum world and consciousness, Quantum Physicists note that atoms are made up mostly of empty space, which contain enormous amounts of energy. In fact, Scientists have found more energy in one cubic centimeter of empty space, the size of a marble, than in all the matter of the known universe. Charles M. Schultz provided a wonderful visual of the energy all around us in his character "Pig-Pen" in the comic strip *"Peanuts."* Pig-Pen carried the dust of his presence around him, defining his space, his environment.

Somehow, in that space, that energy, we are connected and exist. We tend to allow the people who value us as much as we value ourselves, into our space. When we value ourselves it opens the space for others who will value us. Then, amazing things happen and anything becomes possible. Conversely, if we place no value in ourselves, those who share that, take our space and reinforce it to make our lives miserable. So if we change how we value ourselves, we may in turn change the people in our space, and thus our whole experience.

Process this:

> *People will see you as you see you and will help to reinforce what you see. When you change the way you see yourself, others will treat you differently. Try this, if you were to meet yourself walking down the street, who would you see? Is it a true vision of who you are or want to be seen? Many people graduate from high school and go away to college and have a completely different social experience. Everyone in their hometown sees them one way, but their college friends see them differently. In college, the person sees himself differently, and hence he acts and does things differently, and his environment responds in kind.*

For, the relationship between ourselves and our environment is a cooperative process. It is a two-way conversation and a dance of balance. We bond and interact with each other and the Universe, much like chemicals in an equation. So when we allow someone who aligns with us into our space, it enhances and energizes our environment. When our perspective is not based in need, we grow and move. We are invigorated by those around us and we empower them in return. Connected, there is no end to us, our energy, or the space that we create. And when we give out to that space just what we want, with authenticity and truth, it finds its way back to us.

- Do you vibrate harmoniously with the energies and others in your space?

It is up to us to fill our spaces with love, clarity, possibility and inspiration. By honoring self-care and truthfully taking our own vibrations into a unified space with others, we may put aside our illusions in order to remember who we really are. While honoring self-care, this is the true definition of fitting in, a fitting in to ourselves, with awareness. It is not control of the environment, others in the environment or even ourselves in the environment. It is moving, responding and relating to that which vibrates and awakens us. Because we do not fit in when ostracized, bullied or forced into being in a space where others do not recognize and honor our truth. Following the rules does not matter when the rules construct an environment where we fall into 'roles' and do not allow self-care.

Process this:

> *Do we move to fit-in or to express ourselves without limitation? The saying "misery loves company" has taken on new meaning. Some people will go to the greatest lengths to join in your misery if that means they will fit in. Can you imagine when that extends to a community what the environment becomes like? People will go to extremes and will suppress who they are to fit in.*

William Shakespeare, in his play *"As You Like It"* penned: "All the world's a stage, and all the men and woman merely players. They have their exits and their entrances. And one man in his time plays many parts." We are all playing 'roles' and if we don't choose a part for ourselves we will be given one. We may be expected to play martyr, victim, scapegoat, or villain. If we do not define the role we want, the one given will not be satisfying or empowering.

Society is very powerful, alluring and difficult to combat. To keep us from straying from its predefined role for us, it may lead us into many dark alleys of false belonging. We shun our awareness just to belong. In the end it feels unfulfilling, as the space and environment becomes corrupt. No longer is it open and free, allowing growth and understanding. Instead, it becomes filled with foreign vibrations that cause sickness and unhappiness, and basic choices seem to disappear. You may feel stuck within it. The space is not personal space because it is beyond your unique self and your perspective.

The truth is that you are responsible for finding yourself in that space. It was a choice, conscious or not, to step in that space. Now, with awareness you can make a new, conscious choice. As you are responsible for being placed in that space, you have the ability to find your way out of that space. When you find yourself in a space you don't want to be in, it is up to you to say 'No.' Only you need to hear and act upon your 'No,' for by listening and reacting to yourself, your actions and energy create the power of your 'No.'

Process this:

> You put yourself in that space, and that is the bad news. The good news is that you can get yourself out. Expressing "No" is important for you to hear and nobody else. A mother took her daughter for a facial, as a gift. The esthetician had given facials to the mother before. While giving the facial, the esthetician made comments to the daughter that the mother had been a chatterbox and kept her from taking care of her customers. The mother knew the truth of the statement and knowing that the esthetician had used the mother as a scapegoat for her own neglect really got her angry. She decided, NO, she would never go back to the esthetician. She was appalled. She could have called and told her that she was upset, why she was upset and got into a battle with the esthetician. Instead, she made it clear to herself that she heard the no. She called and just cancelled the appointment with a thank you to the receptionist. She had no intention of ever calling again. The mother had to say no, hear no and act on her no. Her actions supported self-care for herself rather than screaming and arguing for someone else to hear her no.

How you choose to act upon your 'No' is up to you and you are responsible and accountable. Once you understand that your perspective is all there is, nobody else can affect you, unless you give them permission. Do what you need to get clarity rather than be angry. Go for a walk, play with a pet, listen to music, or do whatever helps you to get clarity. You have the control. Once you have perspective you can make clear decisions to change your environment (with a new job, new relationship, etc.) or that, for the time being, you will adjust your reactions accordingly (at family gatherings, social events, with community) knowing that it is always temporary.

Similarly, the universe steps up for you when you allow it. A side benefit of having a clear perspective, is that you are open to information you need, in any situation. With a clear perspective, information seems to stream in effortlessly to aid you when struggling to find the truth in any given situation.

•How do you know the truth?

1. If you have history to reflect upon:
History repeats itself. Patterns repeat themselves. People are consistent in the way they act. All of this has nothing to do with you, the reaction is irrelevant to what you do or do not do.

2. If there is no history and the interaction is with someone you have never met:
Be the adult, and act and think like one. Listen to your intuition. You will know if whatever is going on does not feel right within yourself. Step out of the situation. Nothing is personal.

These help you find the truth. What if you know the truth but a bully is in authority? It is difficult to be under the rule of a bully, who makes it hard for you to stay in your space. It could be a boss, the legal system, or any regulating authority, who believes they have power over another person. Perhaps in distracting the bully from his agenda, you can provide an alternative based on your truth. Rather than approaching it from a negative response by saying: "Why are you doing this? Stop that. Who do you think you are? I didn't do anything wrong," choose to be positive. Don't respond negatively or defensively to a negative comment, and don't be predictable and filled with fear.

Process this:

> Bullies thrive when they believe they are in the position of authority. Regulating boards, government positions, law enforcement officials, teachers, and others are breeding grounds for those who like to believe they are in charge. In the child world, it is the ones who are most popular. When you are dealing with a bully, the key for success is to understand what they really are, and simply skirt the issue. What we know about bullies is that when they are left on their own, they cower and will stay in the background. The minute you take away whatever puts them in that perceived position of power, they, in their own mind believe they have no power. They are truly their own worst enemy. If you fully understand this, they will hold no power over you. You can minimize your interaction with them, and they will realize that you are not seeing them as a powerful figure and they will be just as happy to end the interaction as soon as possible. That is the truth.

Tune in to the frequency you desire and your environment will evolve as the right elements fall into place. Albert Einstein said: "Everything is energy and that's all there is to it. Match the frequency of the reality you want and you cannot help but get that reality. It can be no other way. This is not philosophy. This is physics." People are energy and there is a frequency to people. Space exists as a mixture of energy that creates your environment and in turn replicates the reality that is all around you. Your environment is directly related to your perspective.

- You cannot change what people expect of you but you can change what you expect of yourself. Altering your perspective changes your environment and of all that it is constructed.
- What you focus on will bring you the environment and the space, to thrive or not.

Don't be distracted by negativity, illusions of fitting in, and the stories all around you. Instead, ask yourself often:

- What is my truth?

- What is my perception?
- What is my focus?

Process this:

> A small little pizzeria was struggling to survive. A woman joined the crew, and in a short matter of time created a successfully operating environment. She orchestrated the flow of traffic, gave attention to each and every customer, no matter the request, managed every order from start to finish, helped to assemble the meals, and even could be seen inspiring the cooks with her upbeat, energetic personality. With finesse, she even restocked the napkins and tableware, while making sure tables were clean. Her conscientious work ethic spread within the pizzeria making it an enjoyable place to visit, dine in and even work. She created a comfortable environment which clearly spread to the success of the business. People who are conscious of doing that can make a huge impact on this world.

It is time you empowered and elevated your environment with what your truth is, and finally allowed yourself to flourish. Know better and act better, from now on. Be grateful, continue to practice self-care and live with whole hearted presence. Understand how powerful you are. You have created the environment that is around you. By changing what you look for and focus on, you change what shows up for you.

Use the Energetic Invocations for *How do I flourish in my environment?* as an activation tool to expand and organize your energy and move you into healthy, inspiring spaces. Comfortably contemplate them in stillness and silence, allowing the words and vibration to resonate into your cells. The invocations are guidelines to help you on your own journey so feel empowered to personalize them however you see fit.

How Do I Flourish In My Environment Invocations:

1. *I am surrounded by love, support and encouragement consistently in my world within and in my world without.*

2. *My environment is energy and I am interconnected and a part of all that is around me. Another cannot affect my environment unless I allow that energy in.*

3. *The environment can only bother me if I allow it to. By disconnecting those disruptive beliefs, I see the truth of my environment.*

4. *I manifest what I believe so I allow myself the moment to analyze what resonates with me and absorb that cellularly for it to enhance my environment.*

5. *My environment is self-sufficient and expresses itself with consistency allowing abundance and direction.*

6. *Seeing my environment equates to recognizing thought energy moving and with this feeling a knowing occurs, and I allow that to become cellular.*

7. *Recognizing the transparency of sounds in different environments brings me awareness to the resiliency, course and consistency of energy. Sound equates to memories which do not relate to time but rather to feelings.*

8. *Without any judgment, I feel my current environment may be utilized as a learning tool to enhance my growth.*

9. *My environment is created and maintained by my consistency of intent, self-care and awareness.*

Volume 13: Is there a definition for happiness?
Productivity

- How do you define happiness?
- Is it definable?

<u>Process this:</u>

> *Fables and mythology often include tales of magical beings granting wishes as rewards. Most often the person receiving the reward becomes greedy and insatiable for more and more riches and social status, thinking those will finally make her/him happy. Usually the desire becomes their demise, as happiness completely eludes them. If you think happiness is eluding you, are you substituting the same insatiable desire in place of acknowledging what you are content with now, that is currently a part of your life?*

The constant quest for 'happiness' boosts the economy and creates business. As the definition of happiness vacillates between an emotion that makes us feel a certain way and an action we are compelled to undertake, we are trapped into thinking that if we have all we want, we somehow will be fulfilled. We search for happiness and find ourselves desiring and convincing ourselves that if only we had this or that, or when a certain resolution finally occurred, we will then be happy. But are we ever truly happy when we are waiting for that moment to find us? Others seem to find happiness, so why does it continue to elude us?

As we all search for happiness, what are we searching for? A new car, a big house, a fat paycheck, or a size two dress? If we have all that (and anything else we could imagine) is that what will make us happy? Those who appear to have all they want still do not appear happy. Many successful, rich, powerful people who seem to have it all still fall under the influence of drugs, alcohol, or worse.

<u>Process this:</u>

> *Fade in . . . to your partner's perfectly sculpted abs complementing his tuxedo and matching wingtips.*
>
> *Extreme close up . . . on over 25,000 magnificently hand-sewn sequins stretching down your floor-length, pastel designer gown.*
>
> *Pan . . . to your gold stretch limousine with the empty bottle of expensive champagne you just polished off on the back seat.*
>
> *All ready for the red carpet? Places everyone! Quiet on the set! Action!*
>
> *Your movie, your play, your musical, your reality TV show, your name up in lights.*
>
> *Your own piece of Hollywood, Broadway . . . Happy?! Happiness is all around you. Or is it?*

Maybe the secret to happiness lies in a perfect relationship: unconditional love, having a child or being in a wonderful friendship? Sharing your space with others who support and encourage you can enhance your experience here and make the time more enriching. But putting the seeds of your happiness in the hands of someone else or others is not healthy. Would you want to be responsible for someone else's happiness?

The real truth is that nobody can make you happy or unhappy. No one can wish it for you or hand it to you. Conversely, no one can deny it from you or hold it outside of your reach, either. When your own doubts combine with the dysfunctional energy of others, you create distractions which stop you from realizing your own happiness. Because, no one but you can make you anything. With your thoughts, you translate circumstances into what is good and what is bad. Happiness does not depend on these external events and your response is always within your control.

Process this:

> What if you viewed your life as having 3 aspects: physical, social and intellectual? Physical includes your health, weight management, nutrition, activity and overall sense of physical being. Social is all interactions with family, friends, and significant others. Intellectual includes your school work, career, job and intellectual growth and the rewards from it, like finances, being creative, organizing your books and home, etc. When having a difficult time, if you sit down and look at these parts of your life as if on a scale, you can get an overall picture that you are okay because they tend to balance, because at any given point they all fluctuate, one may be at the top and another at the bottom. Realizing that they are always in flux helps you remember that when things really suck in one area, things are better in another. Everyone experiences this and these aspects affect everyone. So what happens when someone asks you if you are happy? What we actually ask ourselves is are we happy even though some one thing or things is/are going on in our life that is/are uncomfortable or challenging. It is a trigger to make you see what you are not happy about rather than focusing on what you are, with gratitude. You tend to forget that things are always evolving. We also tend to forget that nobody has all three aspects positively affecting them in that moment. It is a proven fact that when you tell someone not to look up, they look up, just like when someone asks you if you are happy, you think about why you are not. Once again, the notion of happiness is a trigger that makes us focus on what isn't happy. What if you are content with what is going well, and acknowledge that what might be challenging at the moment is going to move you into different places and is indeed momentary.

In Chinese medicine, the emotion of joy is a pathogen that can cause sickness, like anger or grief. Too much joy is damaging to the heart energy. So this pursuit of happiness leads us down two equally damaging pathways. Either:

1. You have not clarified what makes you happy so you feel something must be wrong: wrong with you or with what you have done.
   You continually try to define your happiness by others' definitions, which leaves you constantly on the hamster wheel searching. You assume everyone else has found happiness and for some reason you

missed it, and this creates a terrible snowball effect that leads you into feelings of lack and/or depression.

Or

2. You look for constant joy, searching excessively.
You join every and any organization, jump on the bandwagon, and are always looking for the next high. Yet this pursuit of joy in excess causes illness. Looking to experience nonstop joy is not only unfulfilling but also can make you sick.

•So, how do you define happiness?

The definition of happiness is the lure of every self-help book, Guru's teaching, and secret philosophy. By convincing you that happiness is out of reach, others bamboozle you into hopelessness. By pursuing another's concept of happiness, you remain tied to a vicious cycle that moves you further into someone else's definition of happiness.

<u>Process this:</u>

If you are quoting Gurus, amassing frequent flier miles by attending Guru workshops, following methodologies developed by Gurus who guarantee to make you happy, or fantasizing about following in the footsteps of a Guru in order to carry on his/her teaching, your identity has been stolen. Actually it has been given away, by you. Stop being lazy and looking for others to fix you. The only secret to uncover is this: You are your own Guru. So help yourself and take back your identity. Do the work for yourself by using whatever experiences, tools, resources, interactions and investigations you need to learn, grow, and move. Decide what to do, how to do it, and with whom. You can have the life you want, and only You can be the Guru you need.

Competition for what we want to acquire and to do, fills our lives. We fear and lack, and when we feel utterly beaten, we look for others to guide us. Because we haven't found happiness, we are perplexed, when it looks like everyone else has. We condemn ourselves and look for happiness in all the wrong places, and guidance from all the wrong people.

We implore others to define what our happiness is. And we believe them, and pay them, because it looks like they are happy so we assure ourselves that they must know what happiness is and can thus tell us where to find it. So, we desperately listen as they tell us that:
- Happiness is having things that appeal to us.

  So, we question what we find appealing.
- Happiness is having an established role in society.

  So, we ponder our role and meditate on why it is not filling us with happiness.
- Happiness is communal and belonging.

  So, we desperately look for a way to fit in but are puzzled when we still don't feel happy.
- Happiness is having a sense of peace and calm.

  So, we search for what is peaceful and calming and distract ourselves with new purchases and pursuits.

We hope the external will fill us with happiness. We incorrectly think that other people's answers will make us happy. We look for anyone, anywhere, to assist us, when, in fact, we are the only ones who can truly help ourselves. By productively inserting ourselves into a space that empowers and encourages us, we could be surrounded with energy that would guide us to happiness. In truly being who we are, while enjoying ourselves, we could find peace and comfort, and love and support, without expectation or judgment. We wouldn't have to pretend to play a role or to fit in. We could remember that whenever we forego who we really are, we are not happy. If we believe we have to live with what makes us unhappy, we are mistaken.

Process this:

A young woman grew up in a traditional Italian family and was brought up to assume the role of caregiver for everyone else in her family and it bled into all her other relationships as well. She cooked for everyone, hosted parties, dropped everything when someone had a problem, made time for everyone and volunteered whenever help was needed. Everyone said what a great girl she was. She did everything to the point of exhaustion. She tried to fix the problems of everyone she met, and wanted to help them feel better and make them happy. The insatiable need she created for others to depend upon her exhausted and depleted her. After deep analysis she came to realize that she put her own happiness on the back burner with the belief that once everyone else was happy, only then could she be happy. So, when do you think she was happy?

There is always another way to be happy, not just someday down the road, but now. Because if you are attaching yourself to someone, something, or some situation that you just must have in order to be happy, you are writing your own prescription for misery. Eastern philosophies tell you that suffering arises from attachment. Interestingly, by waiting for something and wanting it, in order to bring joy into your life, you are attaching yourself to desire. You are creating a vice and becoming an addict. As expectations and assumptions increase, your power and joy decrease. Distracted by unhappiness, you are not connected to all that is happiness. Instead of being open to possibility and wonder, you deny yourself the abundance of happiness that is all around.

Process this:

What are you waiting for to be happy?

You are the only one who can do the work to open up to the idea of happiness. Start by stripping your inner world of all spells, influences, ideas and beliefs. Decide not to judge what you find. Instead, meet it head-on with integrity and compassion. With clarity, direct yourself to see what you really want. Move differently to make it a productive space for what you want. Refrain from judging your description of happiness or comparing it to anyone else's. Your concept of happiness is within yourself, so don't let anyone convince you otherwise.

Because, the only way for you to find happiness is to do the work of mining your inner world. By opening up to this different happiness, you let go of all beliefs and spells. True happiness comes from a place of abundance and creativity. It does not exist in lack or fear, and it does not take from another. The happiness you find is not the happiness of your parents, siblings, friends, cousins or partners. For, You are the only one who knows your own happiness. You claim it, you own it, and most importantly, you are responsible for it. Your happiness is really and truly yours and it is up to you to define it. Because, if happiness is what you truly want, why are you putting up with anything else?

Process this:

> *Because, if happiness is what you truly want, why are you putting up with anything else?*

Use the Energetic Invocations for *Is there a definition for happiness?* as an activation tool to expand and organize your energy and move you into healthy, inspiring spaces. Comfortably contemplate them in stillness and silence, allowing the words and vibration to resonate into your cells. The invocations are guidelines to help you on your own journey so feel empowered to personalize them however you see fit.

Is There A Definition for Happiness Invocations:

1. I strip my inner world of all spells, influences and beliefs, good and bad, to see what I really want. I embrace that difference in my life.

2. I embrace being myself in a supportive environment, free of judgment, guilt and worry, creating a better world, my world.

3. I fully open to all of this in my space and presence, with clarity.

Volume 14: Where do I fuel my presence?
Enrichment

- As you do the work to change and grow, how do you inspire your body, mind and spirit?

You fuel your presence with that which supports and empowers you. Whether it be through relationships, nature, reading, singing, journaling or traveling, you have to make the decision to step out of your comfort zone and into enriching possibility.

Process this:

What empowers you? And how often do you surround yourself in that? A woman loves the feeling of standing in the sun. She only does it when she is at her lowest. If she knows this empowers her, why does she only do it when she needs to change her energy? Why wouldn't she do it every day? Why wouldn't you do what empowers you, consistently?

By enhancing your space, your environment, and yourself, you contribute to your own self-care. You naturally become an advocate for what works for and around you, rather than what doesn't. Because, you are your own responsibility. If you are not looking out for yourself or showing up for yourself, you are not being present for yourself.

And every moment that you are not being aware of your own self-care, you are sabotaging your growth and well-being. There are no excuses, no stories, no mishaps, no diseases and no tragedies of which to convince anyone else. You must experience yourself. Because, you cannot escape yourself, no matter how far away you go.

If you see yourself as part of a situation, you have to step back. You need to let go and become detached and more aware. For, it is not the event that hurts you, but your view of the event which hurts you. If you separate yourself from the situation, you connect yourself with so much more, as things fall into perspective.

- Even science notes that perception is more defined when the background contrasts with what is being seen. A focus aligned with only one detail derived from story will keep you trapped in one reality, bounded by limitation.

<u>Process this:</u>

A painting hangs in a man's living room. Sometimes he sees a European landscape with quaint villas above a calm sea set in the background. Other times he sees a beautiful blue ocean rolling into the horizon with small villas in the background. It is the same picture yet the background helps to contrast what he decides to see, depending on what he places in the background. This is how a person can look at the same picture over and over and constantly see different things. Someone else can come and look at the picture and share other viewpoints that the first person never saw. Art reflects life so what do you see that you didn't see before and what if you changed the contrasts?

Align yourself with where you are by focusing on self-care, in every moment, whether it be at work, rest or play. You fuel your presence by being unequivocally present for yourself. No one else can do that for you, but You. You must practice until this focus becomes second nature. If you are waiting around for someone to rescue you, or take care of you, or even just think of you, you are not living mindfully, with self-care. And it is not your place to make others happy, to supply resources for them, or to create spaces that are warm and comfortable. That will only drain your energy and disconnect you from the All, your constant source. Your presence cannot be active in that kind of space, it simply lies dormant. If you do nothing, nothing changes, and this is not self-care for you.

If dysfunction is around, your goal should be to propel to better spaces rather than sink further into the mayhem with anger. Albert Einstein believed that: "we can't solve a problem while we're in the same level of thinking that created it." So, if you change your level of thinking, your consciousness, you change your reality. In choosing new possibility, you live in a new state, rather than an old one.

It is said that a full-fledged tree exists within a seed, and that the tree itself cannot grow out of it unless it destroys the seed and blooms. You, too, must bloom, regardless of your seed, where your seed is, and who is near your seed. So choose your places wisely, by choosing for You in every space. You are doing all the work, so it is up to you to decide just with whom, where and when you would like to share yourself, your time, and your space.

Process this:

It is now time to think about yourself, free of judgment, comparison or obligation. If the space you currently find yourself in allows you to show up for yourself with power and strength, or inspires you to create more of your own spaces that you wholeheartedly enjoy, then choose it. If it does not, choose wisely. You have done the work so be done with what others think. You are not hurting anyone and now, finally, you are not hurting yourself. A gentleman starts a brand new coffee company. It highlights fair trade with coffee bean farmers and some of the best product coming out of South America. The usual social media and marketing campaigns occur, yet the gentleman begins visiting every retail location to check on the coffee. He is not replenishing it or placing a new display, or giving out free samples. He merely visits it and stands around waiting to see what others will comment. He did all the work so he should be done with what others perceive. They may disparage, complain about the price, or reply positively. Instead of getting caught in others perceptions, he should continue to move in his own space, improving his product, its distribution, and expanding his business. Otherwise, one would ask, what the hell is he doing?

Own your presence, don't be afraid of the truth of who you are. Know what you need and what you want without limitation. Be comfortable with where you are, because if you are not, you should not be there, and you should move and change. You cannot fuel your presence by staying in predictability, by plotting for what others have, by trying to fit in, or by denying who you are with your actions or words.

Whatever you do, think, say or feel, you own. Marshall McLuhan, a Philosopher of communication theory, stated: "the medium is the message." This emphasizes that the means of communicating has more effect than the actual information that is communicated. As such, there is a power to the manner of your communication. It fuels your presence and what is created around you. If you are competitive and envious, you are weakening your power. If you are often tired, exhausted and in survival mode, you are only damaging yourself and your environment. It is not up to you to fix everything and to fill every void with your energy. If you have been conditioning yourself within this kind of cycle it is time to change. Focus on your own business, be mindful of your body and your spirit, connect deeply when and where it is important, entertain the power of your imagination, and use your perception in ways you may never have considered.

<u>Process this:</u>

You are the keeper of your mind. Are you watchful of what is going in and out and being created? If not, who is? If a store owner is constantly running around the town seeing what other stores are carrying, what their prices are and who is going in and out, while his own inventory is getting old and dusty, will it be a surprise when his own store goes out of business? It's time to watch over your own stock and build upon it and decide what direction you want to take. Allow others to do the same.

As Abraham Maslow, a Psychologist, once stated: "If the only tool you have is a hammer, then you start treating everything as if it were a nail." Make awareness your hammer and every present moment a nail waiting to fortify your experience, with mindfulness. Repeat this behavior to form a habit and, as science asserts, you will create circuits within your brain that will treat this habit as an automatic activity. Known as self-directed neuroplasticity, the ability to rewire your brain with your own thoughts, your brain focuses and maps positive thoughts to new neural networks, rather than old ones. This mindfulness helps adjust triggers of old symptoms into better experiences.

When you look at something deeply it becomes a part of you. Physics challenges that when you observe something, like a stone, for example, you are observing the effects of the stone upon yourself. So regain yourself by looking at You deeply, and at what and who is around, with and a part of your existence. How you see and what you see affects your presence.

Process this:

> The stone mentioned above does not change, you change. When you observe something, it changes what you see and feel. It affects you. We have all watched movies and read books or witnessed others' actions which move us, and those feelings stay with us and affect us. When we truly get into the space of what is occurring no matter anyone else's perception, the feeling becomes a part of you. Sometimes you feel things that are not related to you but are related to what you have experienced and seen, good or bad, and they affect you. Knowing that is important.

You fuel your presence as you operate from awareness. As awareness comes from your focus, your truth, and the space you are creating, it exhibits presence in your words and interactions. When that becomes your existence, you increase your power and energy and that space becomes a haven always available to you, to recharge, refuel, and resurge your entire being.

Yet, the where of it is not a physical place, at first, so much as a functioning state of how you are deciding to live. It can become a physical place when it is further enhanced with the sound and vibration of what aligns with you. For when you connect with the whole of your experience, you become intimately present, and so much more alive. There is no need to win, be right or superior to another, or, to have more or fulfill an outrageous reputation. For here, in this space, your ego can relax, feel joy and not struggle in its comparison to others. Because this space is yours and has nothing to do with anyone else. Obstacles blend into opportunities for you to deepen your understanding. Because while in this space, you remain the seeker in search of the energy of what is sought.

Process this:

When you are the seeker, you make a conscious and unconscious effort which aligns you with a vibration that empowers you. Activities that enforce, enhance and enrich, naturally flow into your space. Filled with clarity and productive thought, your space energizes you and allows growth. Where can you go with that?

Our own minds can become our advocates or our villains. We have a choice of how we live and what we choose to focus on, and our words and thoughts can heal or harm us, and others. Only by treating ourselves well and creating beautiful functional spaces for ourselves to grow in, may we nurture and develop. In Chinese theory, the belief is that where thought or intention goes the chi follows, and blood follows chi. Chi is the energy, or life-force, and blood is the physical manifestation of chi. If you take this concept even further it can be analogous to energy transforming into matter. For, 90% of the power is in our awareness and 10% of the rest of our power is in doing the work.

With awareness your space revitalizes, empowers and enriches you. For the challenge is not in creating the space but in staying in that space in times of difficulty. Realize that the space is always available to you, and always accessible to only you. The invocations in this book may help bring all of you into that space, but the work you do will ensure that you confidently stay there. Associating with those who vibrate to your same interests will help you entertain in your space. Visiting nature and other environments that encourage and move you with constructive thought will help you energize ideas rather than form attachments.

Use the Energetic Invocations for *Where do I fuel my presence?* as an activation tool to expand and organize your energy and move you into healthy, inspiring spaces. Comfortably contemplate them in stillness and silence, allowing the words and vibration to resonate into your cells. The invocations are guidelines to help you on your own journey so feel empowered to personalize them however you see fit.

<u>*Where Do I Fuel My Presence Invocations:*</u>

1. *I surround myself with who I am within, and expand it without.*

2. *I breathe with clarity and presence allowing the All to consume me.*

3. I embrace all that occurs as a lesson specifically designed for my benefit.

4. I surround myself in the power of the truth of my presence.

Once you know all of this, the work has been done, and you have awareness. You are now completely responsible for yourself and for what you say verbally and energetically to others. You are responsible for how you treat others, how you think about others, and how you react to others. Now that you know better, you cannot fall back on not knowing. There are no excuses and there is no more blaming. In knowing, you have changed. And in changing, you have changed your world. Now that you have changed your world, step up and change the world.

Part Five – World

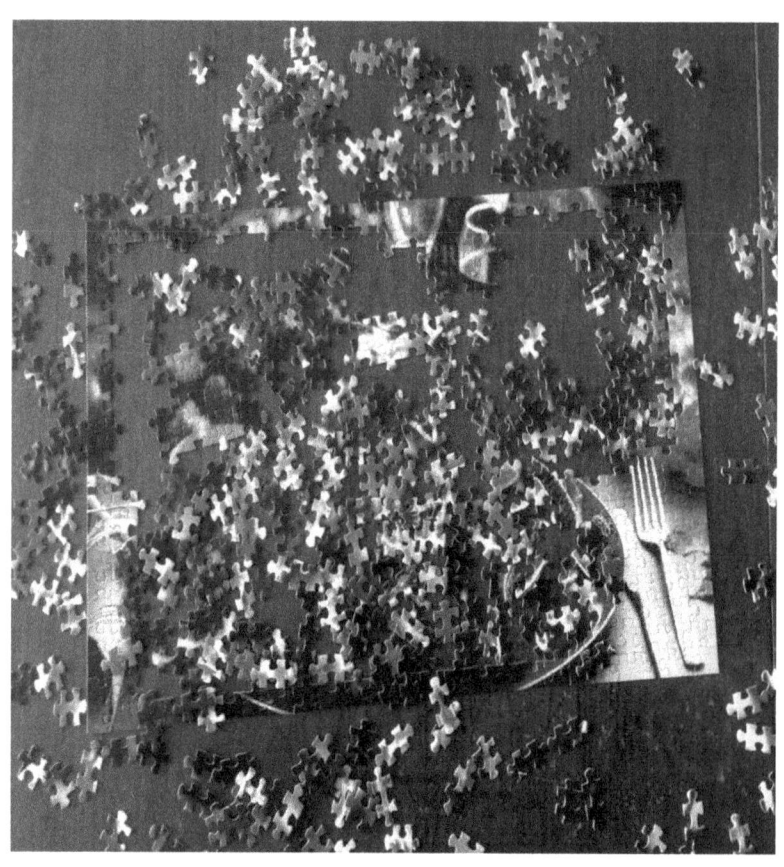

Volume 15: When do I measure time?   *Nurture*

Science tells us that the invention of time helps us feel comfortable in space. Whether it be by a calendar, a clock, a G clef, or years of age, time constructs a known boundary around our experiences, ourselves, and our existence. We hold onto time to construct the usefulness of our experience and thus, give ourselves purpose. By placing everything in the past, present or future, we validate that we exist, as events are recorded, filed, organized and connected. We think we control and own time. Time lures us in by making us resilient as we continue to struggle and fight it. We are constantly restricted by time, yet we are the ones creating the restraint, as time exists as a manmade invention.

We describe time by what happens within it. According to science, it moves with synchronicity as a circle or wheel, and straight ahead like an arrow, due to entropy, when disorder increases. With entropy, as things change they fall into disarray and chaos, moving forward. Eventually the disarray and chaos fall back into order, allowing us to track time. Moving ahead in time, we partition out all our experiences and track their duration, while assigning significance.

As Albert Einstein theorized: "The only reason for time is so that everything doesn't happen at once." If everything did happen at once, how would we cope? How could we construct a story for ourselves and others if so many different characters, actions and places were occurring simultaneously? Science has told us that space and time exist because we do. Without time, how would we relate to others and ourselves and how would we find comfort in the space we are in?

Process this:

> *Imagine no time, no space. Our minds cannot comprehend it. But because our minds can't comprehend it, doesn't mean that it is not so. What possibilities could one conceive of when one has access to all time periods at once, making any time period irrelevant? It may sound like something out of science fiction, but science has found proof, through our study of the cosmos, that time, at different points in space becomes warped, validating that our idea of time is not what we think it is. We may not understand what that means to us, directly, but we cannot deny its validity. We wonder, what else is true and possible?*

If you are thinking about someplace else, you are not being present in where and how you are. You are just measuring time and confining yourself in it. You daydream your way out of a boring lecture and count down the hours when stuck doing something you don't want to do. You hope time passes, yet in missing the moment, you focus on waiting, thinking and planning for some time down the road. If you were present and aware, you could have nurtured the moment, joining with it, and all time would have disappeared.

Science has proven that time is not absolute. Even clocks that tick to measure time vary in their rate and speed because some move fast while others move slowly. Isaac Newton explained absolute time as one that was universal, in space. Yet, Physicists today have shown that the speed of light is absolute, while Einstein showed that time is relative. Depending upon how fast one person's relative motion is from another's, time will pass differently for each. What may seem like one second to one person may feel like a full minute to the other as the time interval between two events is relative and depends on the frame of reference. Einstein also concluded that if you travel faster than the speed of light, you could observe the past, present and future occurring all at once.

- All there truly is, is this moment, right here and right now.

Process this:

> People go to work on a Monday, hoping Friday would hurry up and arrive, wishing their life away. Others spend their time talking about the good old days. At what time are they in the present moment? People predict and live as if the future has already occurred and fantasize how they will play out various scenarios. The best way to affect the future is to be fully present in the now. Science tells us that memories change when we remember them. People reminisce, yet every time they do, something changes in the memory, such as including people who were not ever there and now have become a part of the new memory. When a woman returned to her hometown, she would run into neighbors and old acquaintances. They would tell her how much they remembered certain events and circumstances, and ask her if she ever thinks about them. They would include her in parties, get togethers and laugh with her about what happened. She clearly remembered that she was never a part of it. After a while she started to just say yes she remembered and laughed with them, knowing she was never there. In many circumstances, people want to remember and reminisce about certain things that make them feel a certain way, and by including others, they build comradery. Hence, the memories change... how much time we spend on things that never occurred.

Eastern thinkers, mystics, Quantum Physicists and Buddhists have all prophesized that this moment is all there is. Some people choose to find time important, declaring their place in the past and future, while keeping themselves from the present. Others choose the present moment, being fully there, as experience falls into presence and all definitions of time disappear.

Our choices are in an instant, our feelings are in a moment, and our space is alive, when all the while we are somehow okay. There is nothing to plan for, worry about, fret over, and fight for or decide about, besides being present. By conjuring your world into being each day, you are not caught in the past or the future. When something occurs, and you are present, it is dealt with without thinking. In the present moment, you become infinite. There is no time and within that presence lays power.

Not being confined by time or thoughts of time, allows you to be open and aware. Connected to the moment, you may find others don't have the same awareness or heightened intuition as you because they choose to live in the past or future. They live in fear and worry for what has happened or may never take place. The power of the present moment is not theirs because they are never there.

Process this:

In the present moment, everything is based on just what's in front you. Decisions, ideas, thoughts are not based on what you have known in the past or think will occur in the future. When you do the work in this book, and start to ask questions and really listen to what you find out about yourself, you are in the present moment. It is not scanning the material or skimming it, or multi-tasking when you should be absorbing it. When you multi-task you are not in the present moment. Multi-tasking takes away your time and forces you to turn off the present moment. When you are so absorbed in something and it feels as though time has stopped, or you look up and realize that time has passed, you are in the present moment. When in that space, you feel powerful and limitless, like nothing can stop you. Things appear clearer, you see and hear differently and your brain picks up information it otherwise would not. You have found a relationship with time in the present moment.

Ironically, time is manmade and we have been slaves to time. We applaud time and are in awe of those who seem to have time on their side. As a tool, time is useful to measure when we want to influence what may be occurring in our here and now. By traveling with time and becoming a partner in the spaces between what is known as time, we can gather information and act upon it.

Time travel has been the story of science fiction. Writers, Philosophers and Quantum Physicists have found time to be circular, multidimensional, and full of bends, twists, and turns. Even Einstein said that we are nonlinear beings. As such, we are physical and energetic beings traveling dynamically beyond the confines of time, while using our bodies, minds, and spirits.

Neville Goddard, a teacher of New Thought from the 1950's, used the power of his imagination to envision things occurring in the future and change diagnoses of the past, which affected patients in the present. In *"The Power of Awareness,"* many case studies describe how Goddard envisioned doctors giving healthy verdicts, being stunned when cancerous lumps disappeared, and being puzzled when rare heart conditions healed. By guiding his imagination, Neville Goddard traveled through time to affect the present. He used his imagination and time to create change. If you, too, could visit the past and comfort yourself as a child, or change the negative influence of a suggestion that may now be affecting your health, why wouldn't you? If you, too, could journey to the future for a glimpse of how your successes will be attained, or surround yourself in confidence by tapping into the genuine feeling of what you know then, and transport all this to you now, why wouldn't you?

If you could reinterpret and regenerate your cells by traveling in time and imagining them as they were healthy, like Neville Goddard did, and then take that vision of them into your present moment, would you? By doing that, you could elicit the help of time in your present moment. As all time meets in the present moment, that 'now' could actually be utilized to change any moment of your life that you choose.

Process this:

> *If you allow others to control the feelings you have about yourself and/or time, you are not practicing self-care. How you experience your own time is your decision.*

The time you choose to live in is your own choice. Whether past, present or future, you should never feel guilty about any time that you spend. What you do with your time, how you spend it, and how you value it, is your business. Time is a concept that should not be associated with guilt but with gratitude.

For if you feel pressure to be there for everyone, to put aside your plans and run to where you are needed, you are not nurturing your own present moment. Instead, you are losing time by giving it up to others. If interactions are forcing you to hold onto your time, hiding or hoarding it as you can, then you need to reevaluate your here and now. If you do not give time to yourself, no one else will give time to you.

- For, when you do give time to yourself and then enjoy it with others, you elevate both your experience and theirs, as only you control your perception of time and the present moment.

Use the Energetic Invocations for *When do I measure time?* as an activation tool to expand and organize your energy and move you into healthy, inspiring spaces. Comfortably contemplate them in stillness and silence, allowing the words and vibration to resonate into your cells. The invocations are guidelines to help you on your own journey so feel empowered to personalize them however you see fit.

When Do I Measure Time Invocations:

1. *Time is a manmade thing. I create it, measure it, work with it, and it is on my side.*

2. *All I am is this exact moment, and in this exact moment, all is well.*

3. *When I align my time and energy, there is nothing that can't be healed, fixed or expanded.*

Volume 16: How do I stay balanced in the real world?
Harmony

Balance can only exist when the sum of the parts is considered together because then, the parts integrate as one and harmony is achieved. As a four legged table cannot stand with just three functioning legs, all legs must work competently individually, and in balance with each other. In addition, light cannot exist without darkness, and darkness cannot exist without light. Duality is present because everything has its opposite, but true balance exists only when both extremes are considered.

Process this:

> *There is a power in understanding true duality. Light can only exist in context of its opposite, darkness. So, when we are confronted with a situation or decision and believe we must deal with a difficult event, we need to remember that the direness of any circumstance can only exist if we have access to its opposite. Despite how a situation looks, we have access to both extremes. Most times we analyze our dilemmas with the belief that there is a limited amount of options. If we are concerned that the pending winter will drop ten feet of snow, we must also entertain the idea that we might receive no snow. If an artist is concerned that their work will be shunned and rejected by the art world, they must also embrace the idea that their work will be revered as a masterpiece. So if you have a concern of something occurring, by default the opposite has to be an available option.*

So, all the parts of this book are best absorbed together. If only one part is practiced, and the others are ignored or disregarded, then the effect of this book and the work you do for yourself will not be complete. Balance exists in the connecting, relating and expanding of your experience. When all parts of this book are taken to heart and explored, a balanced experience of change may occur.

Balance demands that all energetic waves and vibrations be in harmony because when they are not, chaos prevails. Science explains that the natural order of things is disorder and chaos, which then leads to order, and subsequently to change followed by more chaos. The *"I Ching,"* known as "The Book of Changes," an ancient Chinese text of divination and wisdom shares that the only thing constant is change. If we use the chaos of change to wake ourselves up, we can move from one extreme to another.

Disorder and change move into balance even within nature. The seasons of the year travel through a cycle, from one to the other. Elements in nature never take more than they need, exhibiting balance in both their consumption and what they offer to the environment. There is a rhythm, a calibrated energy that compensates, naturally.

Process this:

Nature lives with both chaos and order constantly in flux, and so do we. If we embrace that, we learn to move with each just like nature. If we don't we fight a losing battle.

Since balance is in a constant state of flux it is only natural for us to be out of balance. For with imbalance, we find opportunities to grow. This polarity exists everywhere, all around and within us, even with water. Basically the covalent bonds of water do not share electrons equally, so one end of the molecule has a positive charge and the other a negative one. Yet, as a whole, water molecules are neutral and balanced. Remembering that our bodies have a high percentage of water in their cells may help us remember that natural balance and harmony occurs in our bodies all the time.

Some psychologists and new age thinkers claim that if we live from a space of feeling like our dreams and wishes have already been fulfilled we can polarize our minds to enhance their fulfillment and achieve balance. By moving ourselves from sadness and disbelief to joy and belief, we focus more on our desired result occurring. When we realize that the difference between things is merely a degree, polarization becomes clearer. For, it is believed that we can, in fact, move ourselves from one extreme to the other just by our actions and thoughts. By focusing, without doubt, on our wishes being completed and fulfilled, we are transported to that space.

Since we are consistently a work in progress, the most we can hope for is to see the imbalance before we create a story out of it. If we believe that balance is the ultimate destination then we have set ourselves up for failure because every trigger alerts us that our balance is always in flux. By being out of balance, we learn to refine ourselves, our actions, and what we do in order to find a greater space of harmony with ourselves and in our world. We must understand that we came here whole, lacking nothing. Our imbalance does not reflect lack or deficiency. We can only grow and deepen our understanding of ourselves and our environment to the extent that we can question and be open to new experiences, all in the pursuit of balance.

Process this:

A pendulum naturally moves. We are always moving like the pendulum, from point to point, back and forth, one side to another. In this movement, we are not lacking anything, nor do we have too much of anything. Different points on the pendulum do not reflect a deficiency, instead they note balance. When we are in harmony with ourselves, we become in harmony with all around. We then make better choices for ourselves and move forward in a healthier manner.

In Chinese Medicine, when Yin and Yang are in balance, a healthy mind, body and spirit are attained. As Yin and Yang are opposites to each other, and in alternating cycles with each other, they are also dependent upon each other, as they absorb, consume, and transform each other. Yin, as water, is female, deep, wet, dark, cold and still, while Yang, as fire, is male, dry, bright, hot, active, and moving up and out. When Yin and Yang are in balance, there are no deficiencies or excesses. Instead, both are in harmony. Yet, in today's world, many people believe excesses are important. Excess work, alcohol, and money become goals. People work out excessively and consume food and goods in overabundance. Often there is no effort put to balance, unlike in nature, where deficiencies and excesses are worked out harmoniously. It is our own choice to emulate nature and find the balance and harmony within ourselves, our environment, our relationships and our understanding.

Process this:

When we think of being healthy we think of pushing our bodies harder and harder and doing more and more. If we have lived a sedentary life, that too needs balance. Like everything, exercise has to be in moderation. Optimal health is balanced health, not living in an excess.

Balance is a part of our identity just as much as imbalance. *"The Kybalion,"* by Three Initiates, reminds that everything has duality and opposites are two extremes of the same thing with just varying degrees between them. This ensures understanding because even an emotion like love cannot be measured without the help of its opposite, hate. Once aware that we are in one state, our knowledge of the opposite starts to harmonize our reactions, and we integrate balance into our presence.

Process this:

> *Being in harmony is very natural for us when we open up to the possibility. Knowing that all concepts exist with their partners, in duality, like light and dark, happy and sad, tall and short, how do we move ourselves out of one and into another? We start by fully accepting that we have experienced one. Then, we acknowledge that the opposite one exists and we move toward it. We can do this by feeling the opposite and with words and emotions, bringing it into our presence. Then like the pendulum, we naturally move to the opposite of where we have been.*

Our words and intent are powerful vibrations which infuse balance into our thoughts, dreams, and desires. Not only do we say what we mean and mean what we say but also we say what we believe and pay attention to what we habitually tell ourselves and others. By changing our speech and our patterns, we may influence our world, creating the kind of world in which we would like to live.

Use the Energetic Invocations for *How do I stay balanced in the real world?* as an activation tool to expand and organize your energy and move you into healthy, inspiring spaces. Comfortably contemplate them in stillness and silence, allowing the words and vibration to resonate into your cells. The invocations are guidelines to help you on your own journey so feel empowered to personalize them however you see fit.

<u>How Do I Stay Balanced In The Real World Invocations:</u>

1. *All these invocations are equally important and exist in relation to one another.*

2. *As all things exist in relation to their opposites, I experience that there is no extreme that cannot be overcome.*

3. *All things exist for the moment, only.*

Volume 17: What is the truth?   *Awareness*

This is a journey of truth. Your truth.
Can you really handle the truth?

You are too important not to do this work. What if that is the only truth?

In doing this work, you have redefined your truth. So, what is your truth? If you are expecting it to be revealed here, go back and do more work because only you can define your distinct truth. This book can only offer you some generalities surrounding truth.

- Truth is found in the clear and present moment. If you are not in that moment, and not clear and present, then truth is not with you.
- Your stories and others' stories are not truth. They become sounds, vibrations and past thoughts and memories.
- We spend a predominant amount of our lives searching for the truth, so it would stand to reason that most of our lives are filled with untruths since we are searching for what we do not have.
- We do not need anyone to convince us or to stop and force us to adjust our point of view, because the truth is always with us.
- We have forgotten the truth of who we are, the reason we are here and how to take care of ourselves.

By living in truth, we are able to stop the hurtful, dysfunctional cycles that trap us. We can turn the wheel of change and create momentum to empower us to live differently and change our perception, even if it is only our own. There is health, happiness and harmony in the act of stopping an untruth, and moving forward with clarity.

Process this:

> *In all situations, exposing the truth will dispel the horrors of an active imagination. Even when facing the truth is painful, exposing it and breaking it down into manageable pieces will give you the ability to see it and deal with it however you are moved to. Until the truth is exposed, it can continue to cower in the shadows and disguise itself as a completely unmanageable monster. A little girl has a reoccurring nighttime fear that someone or something is at her bedroom door. She does everything she can to keep whatever it is behind the door. It isn't until she gathers the courage to peek out the door and fully look at what is out there does she expose the truth and the realization that nobody and nothing is actually there. She may need to do this a few times, but each time her resolve becomes more concrete. Once the truth is exposed, it destroys the unmanageable monster lurking outside her door, which initially had appeared to be unconquerable.*

Truth exists side by side with awareness. When you move into the space of awareness:

1. You have understanding.
   With awareness comes real power over this world of illusions as you comprehend more about how to live with the illusion rather than in it.

2. You create new situations in which to live and to grow.
   Remind yourself that beliefs are not a knowing. By seeing the truth, you remove yourself from unhealthy situations and lack. The truth will always resonate with the highest and best intentions for you.

3. To understand more you must make an effort to live with awareness and maintain it.
   If you are troubled by another or by an event, it is most important not to react. By seeking and using all your resources to get to clarity you will have a stronger sense of self. Others' awareness is not your responsibility. Your responsibility is to yourself.

Forcing your awareness on others is not just futile, but also irresponsible.

Process this:

You are here, are you ready?

Once you have awareness, you are no longer able to deny it. You are no longer part of the crowd and you cannot hide behind the excuse of not knowing any better. You do know better. If you choose to be unaware, understand that is the choice you are making.

So, take the time now to create your own energetic invocations for *What is the truth?* Use them as an activation tool to expand and organize your energy and move you into healthy, inspiring spaces. Comfortably contemplate them in stillness and silence, allowing the words and vibration to resonate into your cells.

Once you know that much has been lost in your own translation, you now fully understand that to change the world you have to change your world. It is about how you act and interact, and how you proceed. It is time for all of us to change our world.

Final Words *Authenticity*

Let's remember a few things:

Who is the one person you can change? You.

Did you know that? Of course you knew that. Everyone knows that.

So, why are you looking outside yourself to fix your problems? You change your world by changing yourself.

All the answers are inside of you. It is up to you to do the work. This book shakes you up so you find the answers, for yourself.

When you get to the truth, there is sense. If you try to live your life with the rules and conditions you've been told and given, not much makes sense.

You are important. You do matter. This book provides a pathway to the truth.

Take the journey and do the work, for yourself. Because when you change yourself, you change your world. And the only way to change the world, is to change your world.

You are here, still. We are too. But we are not willing to empathize with you. Nor should you, with us. Empathy is enabling. Authenticity is empowering. And it is all about authenticity.

Process this:

> *I know I am fully capable of doing, creating, handling everything and anything with power and grace. It just is. It's part of my knowing. I allow all creative enhancements to my life, to enjoy even more, without limitation, all the Universe has to offer me. In return, I can continue to grow and give more of myself, without hesitation.*

Life is a process and how you carry yourself through that cycle is your business. If you do the work, you find answers within yourself and all around you. What matters is what you believe and what you think about yourself. Your power is derived with a clear connection to yourself, yet everyone you meet will trigger you, and your reaction is only symbolic of your power or the power you give away.

Ironically, the most important rule of life is to get out of your own way. There is nothing for you to do, and that certainly includes drawing yourself into your own and other people's drama. By disconnecting from storylines, triggers, roles and responsibilities, you will feel the ultimate connection. Through disconnection there is connection. When you get this, you realize anything you do to someone else you do to yourself.

Authenticity is related to this disconnection. When you disconnect you are left with authenticity. And in that authenticity you may trust that:

- You change and affect yourself.

- If your intent is truly for your best, it stands to reason that nobody else will be hurt, unless they have a selfish expectation of you.

- Nothing is personal because what others say and believe about you is only a reflection of themselves.

Trying to change that is futile. You cannot directly affect anyone but yourself.

•The best way to affect anyone is simply to be yourself, with no judgment or expectation and then, to be the example.

So now you have done all this work. The best thing you can do is bring a full, healthy, powerful you into the world. If you can do that then you are being true to yourself. But remember that at the end of the day, you also have to live with yourself.

About Julie Bonetti and Susan Barbaro writing this:

Between the two of us, we have had a lot of similar experiences, with families, friends and interests and in many companies and continents. While the flavor of our lives is different, our focuses and intents are the same. When our paths intersected, we found that we balanced and counterbalanced each other. Yet, we agreed that it was time to pass on all that we had learned.

This book you hold spans years of living, loving and learning, in good and bad times, with dysfunction, heartache, failure, success, opportunity and wonder, all around. We wrote this book together because it was the kind of book we both wanted to read. And in writing it together, we trudged through every part, documenting perception, beliefs, chaos and what we found we knew and did not know. And in doing that, we found our truth. Every step of the way, we did the work, and we continue to do the work. Our lives have changed and our world has changed. But that is our business.

Your life is your business. So mind it with self-care. You are important. You have the answers. Change is life and the only person you can change is you. Do the work and show yourself what you know. Reveal your truth. Be courageous, be brilliant, be amazing, and be limitless enough, for yourself.

From the Authors:

If you have any interest in things other than people's stories, complaints and drama, and feel that there is something else out there, you're right, there is. And that's where we are.

Social media, television, movies, other self-help books are unfulfilling. They just perpetuate an empty feeling. If you are interested in what everyone else is doing, keep supporting them. Yet, if you are interested in accessing something else within yourself and all around you, our books help to open the door to magick, science, creativity, and psychic ability.

We work with energy. What does that mean?

Everyone wants to talk to us or be in our conversations. So, we wrote about what we know and have experienced. If you want to be in our conversations, listen to our podcasts. Otherwise, read our books, that's where the energy is.

Find our books on our Amazon Author pages and via the list at the front of this book or here: https://fanlink.tv/EiAlliance

Find our archived podcast shows everywhere:
"So What! Now What?"
"Write, Now! with Julie B"
"Your Presence Is Required"
"Let's Talk About Energy, Ours & Yours"
"The Kybalion: A Conversation"
"Ancient Texts – The Genealogy of Energy"
"Oprah! Can You Hear Me? Oprah vs. Donald 2020 and Beyond!"

Find out about our BLOTCH© cards and ebooks, and how Blotch© creates the voice, to say, and hear, that it's okay to be different and not fit in. Blotch© supports others, to be just who they are through his fun, ironic and witty viewpoint.

Follow "Ei Alliance" on:
Facebook, Twitter, Instagram, Spotify, Medium, and YouTube

EnergeticInvocations@gmail.com

www.ingramcontent.com/pod-product-compliance
Lightning Source LLC
Chambersburg PA
CBHW050111170426
43198CB00014B/2535